Victorian
Lancashire

Victorian Lancashire

Edited by S.P.Bell

David & Charles : Newton Abbot

0 7153 6213 5

© S. P. Bell and contributors 1974

Set in 11/13 IBM Journal
and printed in Great Britain
by Biddles Ltd Guildford Surrey
for David & Charles (Holdings) Limited
South Devon House Newton Abbot Devon

Contents

Contents

Preface

In the last decade a great deal of work has been done for higher degrees on all aspects of nineteenth-century British social history, much of which, surprisingly, remains unpublished and thus inaccessible to the general reader. This volume has been compiled from theses which, with the exception of that by Smith, have not been published in any form before.

It is hoped that the common themes of Lancashire·and the nineteenth century will give this collection not only a local interest but also a wider appeal, especially as it is now generally accepted that the national picture can be understood only from local 'segments' built up into 'regional mosaics'. Nor should it be forgotten that, as Eric Midwinter has pointed out, the history of Lancashire is 'greater in quality and significance than that of many a nation'. Thus the study by A. T. McCabe on the standard of living and that by J. Lea on religion and the working classes are both important contributions to continuing debates, while the chapters by A. F. Davie and R. L. Greenall are both original contributions to our knowledge of county and municipal administration respectively. The remaining chapters, on the police (W. R. Cockcroft), the

Preface

press (P. J. Lucas), entertainment (M. B. Smith) and entrepreneurs (J. H. Fox), are representative of the wide variety of
historical research being carried out in English universities
into relatively unexplored aspects of nineteenth-century
social history.

I should like to thank all those people who helped me to
track down my contributors in the first place, and in particular to Professor H. J. Perkin of Lancaster University, who
made many helpful suggestions at the beginning. To him, and
of course to my eight contributors, I am most grateful.

Salford, Lancashire   S. P. Bell

Chapter One

The Administration of Lancashire, 1838-1889 [1]

A. F. Davie

Before the establishment of county councils in 1889 the administrative work now performed by them was carried out by the justices of the peace in the courts of quarter sessions in the intervals between or at the end of the judicial proceedings. In most counties four quarter sessions courts were held each year, but in Lancashire sixteen were held annually, four each at Lancaster, Preston, Salford and Kirkdale near Liverpool. For some time, however, it had been found difficult to transact county business at so many different places. From about the end of the seventeenth century, therefore, the Lancashire justices had been accustomed, during the assizes held at Lancaster, to attend a meeting convened by the high sheriff called 'the Sheriff's Board', at which they transacted business relating to the county at large. Eventually it became difficult to arrange these meetings, so they were abandoned around the middle of the eighteenth century. Then, from 1787 until almost the end of the century, a special adjournment of the quarter sessions at Preston was made annually in July to transact all administrative business relating to the county. For years the justices of the hundred of

Lonsdale vigorously opposed the holding of this special
adjournment at Preston instead of at Lancaster, the county
town, situated in their hundred. This drove the justices of the
rest of the county into promoting a bill in Parliament which,
as the Lancashire Sessions Act, became law on 21 June 1798.

This act empowered the Lancashire justices to hold a Court
of Annual General Session at Preston on the Thursday following 24 June every year, and to adjourn it if necessary. It was
not, of course, a selective body, as all the justices for the
county could attend if they so desired. At this annual general
session or its adjournments, they were given powers to deal
with the erecting, building, enlarging, altering, maintaining
and regulation of gaols, houses of correction, bridges and all
other public buildings and works, the expenses of which were
chargeable to the county rates. Likewise, the power of nomi-
nating, electing, appointing, removing and paying the salaries
of the county treasurer and all other public officials whose
salaries were payable from the county rates was given to the
annual general session. All business relating to the assessing of
the county rates and the passing of accounts, hitherto done
at the quarter sessions, was now to be determined at the
annual general session; but the county rates, so assessed, were
to continue to be levied at the quarter sessions. No other
county in England followed the example of Lancashire in
legally securing a court to deal with county administrative
business. A single meeting in June was never sufficient for
the conduct of the administrative business of the county,
however, and by 1838 at least five meetings were held per
year, each meeting appointing the date of the next. With so
many meetings annually the Court of Annual General Session
became known as 'the annual general sessions'.

Lancashire was not only a county but also a county palatine,
in which the holder or owner had the same sort of powers
that the king had in his kingdom, with courts parallel to those
at Westminster and with his own administration within his
county. In this way, Lancashire possessed its own Court of

Chancery and, until 1873, its own Court of Common Pleas. By the nineteenth century, however, the fact that Lancashire was a county palatine made little difference in its administration compared with that of other counties.

At the head of the county there was, as today, a lord lieutenant, who had charge of the military forces in the county, the cost of providing or renting storehouses for the safe custody of arms and equipment being a charge on the county rates. As in most counties, the lord lieutenant was also *Custos Rotulorum*, the nominal custodian of all judicial and other documents, the actual custodian being a deputy called the clerk of the peace. In Lancashire, however, apart from occasionally transmitting documents from a secretary of state or another lord lieutenant to those justices attending the annual general or quarter sessions, the lord lieutenant had very little to do with the civil administration of the county.

Another officer of the county was the sheriff or high sheriff, whose duties were chiefly in connection with the assizes and quarter sessions. On the administrative side the control of the county gaol at Lancaster was in his hands, but the effective administrative control was exercised by the annual general sessions and its committee of visiting justices. He remained, however, solely responsible for the carrying out of death sentences. There were also the county coroners, who held office for life. These were elected by the freeholders of the county but their travelling expenses, fees (salaries after 1860) and the expenses of the inquests they held were met from county funds.

The clerk of the peace was an important official in whose office all documents concerning the courts together with registers, bonds and returns of various kinds were deposited. At the quarter sessions he was responsible for the correct ordering of the court. In Lancashire, by 1838 this office had long been a patent office in the gift of the Crown. The patent holders appointed a deputy, shared with him the salary allowed from the duchy funds and left him to conduct all the legal business of the county. From 1796 to 1879 the different clerks of the peace each made a 'deputation' of their authority to a firm of Preston solicitors — Gorst, Gorst and Birchall — who, as deputy clerks of the peace, carried out the duties of the office and were generally referred to as the 'deputy clerks'. In 1879 the office of clerk of the peace became a salaried one, although the appointment to the post did not lie with the county justices but with the chancellor of the Duchy of Lancaster. The deputy clerk of the peace (clerk of the peace after 1879) was a person of great importance not only in the administration of justice within the county but also in its civil administration. At the annual general sessions he was the legal adviser of the justices attending and their chief executive officer. Nevertheless he was not a county officer and was quite independent of the county justices.

Besides officers of the county there were officers for each hundred (or county division), elected annually at the appropriate court of quarter sessions. They were termed high constables to distinguish them from parish constables, who, by the nineteenth century in Lancashire, had become salaried county officials rather than officers of the hundred. They performed two main functions, one judicial and one administrative. On the judicial side they were the channels through which passed all orders, warrants and precepts from the quarter sessions to the parish officials. On the administrative side they supervised the making of all returns and received, from the overseers of the poor or the parish constables, the sums due by way of county rates, transmitting these to the county treasurer. Up to 1844 there were fourteen high constables in Lancashire, four for the hundred of West Derby and two each for the other five hundreds (Amounderness, Blackburn, Leyland, Lonsdale and Salford). The establishment of a county police force in 1839 soon rendered them superfluous in a judicial connection and when, under the County Rates Act of 1844, the rate precepts (notices) were in future to be sent to the boards of guardians of the poor

The Hundreds of Lancashire

law unions, high constables ceased to be necessary for administration; their salaries ceased in 1845. One unsalaried high
constable continued to be appointed for each hundred to deal
with riot damages, but in 1869 this power was transferred to
the chief constable of the county constabulary, and high
constables were no longer appointed.

Thus, although Lancashire in 1838 was still, to some extent,
administered by the officers of the county, and in certain
matters affecting the hundreds of the county by the courts of
quarter sessions, the act of 1798 had virtually placed the
county administration under the Court of Annual General
Session, which dealt almost wholly with administrative
matters. In 1838, however, four Lancashire boroughs —
Bolton, Manchester, Liverpool and Wigan — secured separate
courts of quarter sessions, which placed them outside the
jurisdiction of the county justices, while in 1887, Blackburn and
Oldham also became quarter sessions boroughs. The Court of
Annual General Session had no authority to levy county rates on
these quarter sessions boroughs, but the boroughs remained
liable for contributions towards county costs in respect of
general purposes, asylums and bridges. These contributions
were secured by means of orders by the county treasurers on
the respective corporations. The actual area, therefore, administered by the annual general sessions after 1838 was the
geographical county less the area and population of the
quarter sessions boroughs.

Although by 1838 the Court of Annual General Session
had been administering Lancashire for forty years, little
change had been made in its procedure since it had been first
formed.[2] As a court it was established, and as a court it continued to function. At its meetings the justices could raise
any matter that interested them and could speak for as long
as they liked with the result that, not infrequently, the proceedings degenerated into simultaneous discussions between
different groups. The only matters fixed were the procedures
for dealing with the accounts and the making of appointments,

while the only permanent committees were statutory ones for the prisons and the county asylum. It was also necessary at every meeting to move that one of the justices present should be chairman for that meeting. From 1826 to 1850, however, T. B. Addison, Recorder of Preston and Chairman of Preston quarter sessions, was moved to the chair for most but not all meetings.

The two main meetings of the annual general sessions were the legally fixed June meeting and its adjournment in September, but three or four additional adjournments were always necessary. Mr Addison, as a matter of personal convenience, arranged these extra adjournments for the first days of the quarter sessions at Preston. Opposition soon developed after 1840 to this conducting of county business during quarter sessions time since it often caused delay in the transaction of judicial business and since, because of the small attendance of justices, these adjourned meetings were dominated by the Preston area justices. Complaints were also made about the dealing with matters without previous notice of motion and some irregular subsequent action over resolutions passed. Disapprobation of the way in which the county treasurer handled county finance and strongly expressed disapproval of the size, cost and calibre of the new county police swelled the volume of criticism levelled at the county justices.

Apart from settling for a smaller police and differential rating for police costs, no further action was taken over these complaints until 1849. In that year a committee appointed for the purpose prepared a series of standing orders for the annual general sessions which, after being amended in detail by these sessions, came into force in 1850. These standing orders provided for an order of proceedings at the meetings of the annual general sessions together with the now well recognised rules in connection with the movement of resolutions and amendments and the right of reply. Agendas were to be issued to all the acting justices of the county and these had to be accompanied by all notices of motion, which had to be sent to the deputy clerk of the peace in writing fourteen days before the date of a meeting. The exact duties of the county treasurer were set down together with the procedure to be adopted in the appointment of county officers. A chairman was to be appointed yearly, but it was not until 1860 that a vice-chairman was also appointed. Standing committees, each of which had to appoint annually a chairman and vice-chairman, were also to be appointed. The number of meetings of the annual general sessions was fixed at four: the main sessions in June, the adjournment in September and two adjournments to continue to be held on the first day of the January and Easter sessions of the Preston quarter sessions. Subsequently the particular standing order was amended to allow these adjournments to be held on the days before the quarter sessions commenced.

In the same year, 1850, in which these standing orders introduced order and precision into the proceedings of the Court of Annual General Session, the county justices appointed a new county treasurer who was also to introduce order and much greater precision into the accounts of the county. Taken together, these two developments enabled the justices attending the Court of Annual General Session to begin something of a new era in the administration of the county. This was very timely; for in the following years determined efforts were made on behalf of the poor law boards of guardians to secure the setting up of county financial boards, composed partly of justices and partly of representatives of the poor law unions to administer the financial affairs of counties. Indeed it was a meeting representative of the Lancashire boards of guardians which initiated the campaign and promoted abortive bills in Parliament to secure legislative enactment for these boards.

From the earliest years of its existence the Court of Annual General Session had made use of committees. Appointing a committee was an obvious way to secure, at greater leisure, a

more thorough consideration of some matter for which the
annual general sessions as a whole could not spare time. The
practice of appointing such committees continued after the
reforms of 1850 and in time they became styled 'special
committees' to distinguish them from standing committees.
The special committees remained in being until the reports
which were usually required on their inquiries had been
received by the annual general sessions and action taken upon
them. The new departure in this connection was the appointment in 1850 of standing committees. These were permanent,
but their members were subject to yearly election and their
spheres of action were delineated in the standing orders if
not subject to regulation by any act of Parliament. Immediately, the General Finance Committee and the district finance
committees, all constituted previously, and the long established committees of visiting justices for each prison and the
lunatic asylum became standing committees, and new standing committees were formed as the need arose.

A committee for examining and auditing the public accounts
of the county had been elected yearly since 1819 but had
never worked satisfactorily because of the poor attendance
by members. In 1845 it reported its inability to deal with
these accounts in the time allotted, so that a special committee
was thereupon appointed to inquire into the keeping and
examining of county accounts and the main recommendations
of its report were approved and effected. To deal with county
finance a two-tier system was created. Henceforth at the mid-
summer quarter sessions at Lancaster, Preston, Salford and
Kirkdale a district finance committee was to be elected annually to examine quarterly all accounts from within the sessions
area and to issue orders on the county treasurer for the payment of all bills allowed. They were further required to prepare and submit to the respective courts of quarter sessions
an estimate of expenditure in the area for the ensuing quarter.
Then at the adjourned annual general sessions in September a
general finance committee was appointed annually consisting

17

of two members from each district finance committee.

It was not until the appointment of a new county treasurer in 1850 that this new system became really systematised. Then all officials were required to make up quarterly accounts and present them in person to the appropriate district finance committee. Each district finance committee held eight meetings per year, at four of which the accounts of the coroner or coroners for the sessions area concerned were examined and recommendations were made as to their being allowed by the quarter sessions. At the other meetings the return of fees made by the inspectors of weights and measures were examined and ordered to be paid to the county treasurer. Their bills of expenses were allowed and, together with the amounts of their salaries, were ordered to be paid by the county treasurer. The accounts of the bridgemaster(s) for both county and hundred bridges were also examined and allowed. In addition their financial requirements for the ensuing quarter were examined, and if approved, the particular bridgemaster was authorised to apply for the amount so approved at the next appropriate quarter sessions. When standing committees were first formed the annual general sessions decided against forming a bridge committee because in Lancashire the number of hundred bridges (498) far exceeded the number of county bridges (43), and in each hundred the bridgemaster for hundred bridges was always appointed surveyor of county bridges. All questions of repairs of county bridges as well as of hundred bridges were left to the quarter sessions. In turn the quarter sessions deputed much to the district finance committees.

The district finance committees found it impracticable to prepare estimates of expenditure for each ensuing quarter. Therefore they adopted the plan of making two separate sets of estimates, one for a 'quarter' from 1 June to 28 February following and another for the period 1 December to 31 August, in accord with the overlapping periods for county rates. These estimates were submitted to the next court of quarter sessions and, if there approved, passed on to the annual general sessions.

These committees suffered from poor attendance, and for the effective examination of accounts relied much on their part-time clerks. With the appointment of a county auditor in 1864 their duties in connection with accounts became supervisory. Nevertheless, they continued to perform the useful function of checking local officials, besides being advisory and administrative committees of the quarter sessions in respect of their non-judicial functions.

The General Finance Committee of the annual general sessions was entrusted with three functions — to keep the expenditure of the county constantly under review; to prepare and submit to the annual general sessions estimates of the probable expenses for the ensuing year; and to examine, audit and settle the accounts of the county treasurer. The committee employed a part-time accountant to assist in the preparation of estimates and, in point of fact, he did all the auditing of the accounts with the exception of the internal accounts of the asylums, which were examined by a subcommittee of the respective committees of visitors. All accounts, except those for the separate hundreds, were signed by the county treasurer as presenting them, by the part-time accountant as having audited them and by all eight members of the General Finance Committee as having allowed them. The accounts for hundred bridges were in two separate forms. Accounts were kept by the county treasurer with each hundred separately, balancing the rates levied for hundred bridges against sums advanced to the bridgemaster concerned. In each case another account was presented by the bridgemaster of each hundred, balancing cash received against actual payments.

In 1864 a county auditor was appointed but it was felt that the county treasurer's accounts ought to be audited by an independent auditor. Therefore a part-time appointment continued to be made on a yearly basis and the yearly audit of the main county accounts was carried out by this part-time auditor and not by the county auditor. That official acted as clerk to the general and the district finance committees and examined all bills and accounts including those of the lunatic asylums with the consent of the respective committees of visitors.

Twice each year the General Finance Committee presented estimates of expenditure to the annual general sessions. These estimates covered two overlapping periods — from 1 June to 28 February and from 1 December to 31 August — which was to allow for the time lag between the rates being laid at the annual general sessions, then levied at the quarter sessions, and finally collected. This committee held at least eight meetings per year at which the business transacted chiefly concerned county accounts. At every meeting the county treasurer was required to reveal his balance at the county bankers, and quarterly his petty cash disbursements were examined and allowed. The whole business connected with county printing and advertising was placed under the control of the General Finance Committee, who also authorised all expenditure in respect of legal proceedings and petitions to Parliament. On questions referred to it — such as loans to be raised or salaries to be paid — the recommendations were almost invariably adopted and passed as resolutions by the annual general sessions.

The General Finance Committee was the most important of the standing committees. In addition to financial affairs it dealt with matters of wider concern which should have been referred to the General Purposes Committee; and for a time it superseded the Parliamentary Committee in dealing with action to be taken over parliamentary bills. Its eight members were always members of every other committee and several were usually chairmen of other standing committees. Just as the district finance committees were the chief advisers to the quarter sessions, so the General Finance Committee was the chief adviser to the annual general sessions, but that body had the final word on all important matters.

In Lancashire the power of the justices to make and levy rates was interpreted in the light of the peculiar circumstances of the county. The general county rate levied on the administrative county was a rate to cover what was regarded as 'general purposes'. This comprised the expenses of Lancaster Castle Gaol, the costs of prosecutions at the assizes and quarter sessions, the conveying of prisoners to prisons and hulks, the apprehending and passing of vagrants, the salaries and expenses of county officials and a few miscellaneous charges. To these were added, after 1855, the costs of the erection and maintenance of militia storehouses and, after 1866, the expenses connected with the Diseases of Animals Acts. Entirely separate rates were levied for the county asylums and for county bridges, because the charter boroughs of Clitheroe, Lancaster, Preston, Wigan and the old township of Liverpool were not rated for county bridges. Lastly a general county police rate was levied to meet the expenses of the headquarters at Preston.

Besides county rates there were hundred rates. The total expenses of the houses of correction at Preston and Kirkdale were met by a separate rate on the five hundreds excluding the hundred of Salford. That hundred was rated separately for the Salford Hundred House of Correction and separately again to pay for the salary of the chairman of Salford quarter sessions. After 1880 the hundreds of Amounderness, Blackburn and Leyland were also rated separately in respect of the salary of the chairman of Preston quarter sessions. Each hundred was rated separately for its hundred bridges, for riot damages within the hundred and, after 1878, for a contribution towards the maintenance of the main roads in the hundred. Each police division was rated in respect of the expenses of the police stationed within its borders. All boroughs having their own police forces were exempt from county police rates. Boroughs policed by the county constabulary did not pay police rates but were served with orders for the amounts due by the county treasurer. To complete the picture of different area rating, the division of Manchester after 1844 paid a separate rate for the expenses and salary of its stipendiary magistrate.

These rates, having been laid by the annual general sessions and levied on the county hundred or division of the county by the appropriate court of quarter sessions, had then to be collected. Up to 1844 the churchwardens and overseers were required to pay the county rate out of the poor rate for their parishes. The high constables of the hundred received the county rate from these local officials and paid the whole sum to the county treasurer. Then the County Rates Act of 1844 directed that the precepts for the collection of these rates should be sent to the boards of guardians, who were charged to send the aggregate sums collected from the parishes of their respective unions to the county treasurer. The county rate was still to be paid out of the poor rate collected by the overseers of the poor. Thus, although the county rates were still levied on the hundreds, the poor law unions had replaced the hundreds as the median collecting units and the poor law union clerks had replaced the high constables as the links between the overseers of the poor and the county treasurer. No further change was made, the county justices recoiling from the idea of building up a headquarters staff at Preston.

County rates necessitated valuation of all property from time to time, with the result that the Lancashire justices carried through valuations in 1815, 1829 and 1841. These were supervised by a deputy clerk of the peace to ensure that the valuation was made on one uniform principle. Returns of the full annual value of the estates and property assessed to the poor rate were made in writing by the overseers of the poor for every parish or township to the justices in petty sessions. The county treasurer assisted these justices in ascertaining the correct annual value. The returns from the fifteen petty sessional divisions were then sent to the annual general sessions at Preston. There the justices made small changes in the valuation of thirty-nine townships before allowing and putting into force the new valuation.

In 1849 the first County Rate Committee was elected at the annual general sessions under the provisions of the County Rates Act. It consisted of eleven members, two each from the Lancaster and Preston quarter sessions, three each from the Salford and Kirkdale quarter sessions and with a prominent justice as chairman. Uncertainty as to whether or not county administrative and financial boards were to be established led this committee to abandon the attempt to make a new valuation. Parliament then consolidated the law on county rates into a single statute — the County Rates Act of 1852 — which provided that a county rate committee should consist of one justice from each petty sessional division in a county. Pursuant to this provision the second County Rate Committee of nineteen members — one justice from each petty sessional division — was appointed at the annual general sessions held in September 1852 and authorised to make a new valuation of the county. A deputy clerk of the peace was appointed clerk and the county treasurer accountant to the committee. As the precepts for rates were now sent to the boards of guardians, the returns were required from the clerks of the thirty poor law unions in the county. These returns were made direct to the County Rate Committee and the valuation thus arrived at was confirmed and adopted at the annual general sessions held in April 1854. This County Rate Committee was reconstituted in 1859 but contented itself with revising the 1854 valuation.

In 1862 union assessment committees appointed by the boards of guardians from among their own members were authorised for every poor law union. The boards of guardians consisted not only of elected members, but also of the justices resident in the respective unions as *ex officio* members. The Union Assessment Committee Act of that year laid down that each such committee should be composed of at least one-third of these *ex officio* members. This meant that county justices were always represented on these committees.

In a valuation, the returns were still made from the overseers of the poor for each parish to the clerks to the guardians and from these to the County Rate Committee. The union assessment committees assisted in the making of county valuations and made a yearly review of the valuations in their union. No further change was made and new valuations were carried through in 1866, 1870, 1877 and 1884.

The County Rate Committee was a statutory committee which the justices at their annual general sessions were bound to appoint. It was not made a standing committee; though it was appointed yearly, it remained in being until it was decided to have a new valuation, whereupon a new committee ' was appointed. Members of the committee were not really elected. From the time when the committee consisted of one justice from each petty sessional division, it was the practice at those sessions to find a justice willing to serve and to forward his name to the annual general sessions for appointment. The County Rate Committee carried through the different valuations of rateable property in the county and dealt with objections against assessments, but the valuations and any reductions or increases made in any rateable values had to be confirmed and allowed at the annual general sessions.

Lancashire had one county gaol and three houses of correction[3] and in 1850 the committees of visiting justices for these prisons became standing committees of the annual general sessions. The administration of these institutions differed somewhat as between Lancaster Castle Gaol and the houses of correction. Theoretically, the gaol was in the custody of the high sheriff, but little was heard of him in the oversight and management of that prison. He remained responsible for the safe custody of debtors in the prison and his permission was still necessary for their removal to another gaol. The committee of visiting justices for the gaol was elected yearly at the annual general sessions, and after 1865 its membership was confined to the justices of the hundred of Lonsdale in which the gaol was situated. The visiting justices were required to visit and inspect the gaol regularly — a rota of two justices performed this duty monthly. The visiting committee dealt with minor matters of discipline; it could order repairs not exceeding £200 and, if so authorised by Lancaster quarter sessions, could make appointments to minor posts. All additions to the staff, the dismissal of officers, changes in diet and orders on the county treasurer in respect of payments had to be authorised at Lancaster quarter sessions.

Committees of visiting justices were also appointed yearly at the annual general sessions for Preston House of Correction and Kirkdale House of Correction at Liverpool. The functions of these committees were similar to those of the Lancaster Gaol Committee, but Preston quarter sessions played a lesser part in the affairs of Preston House of Correction than was the case at Lancaster, and Kirkdale quarter sessions had little to do with the house of correction there. The visiting justices, the governors, the chaplains and the surgeons were all required to present yearly reports to the annual general sessions. The appointment of all senior officers and decisions on all matters of importance were made at the annual general sessions. The Prisons Act of 1877 'nationalised' all local prisons.[4]

In the case of the Salford House of Correction, the prison authority was legally defined as the justices of the hundred of Salford, but by agreement the committee of visiting justices was formally appointed by the annual general sessions each year. That committee confined itself to inspection and minor matters. All other matters in connection with the prison were dealt with at Salford quarter sessions and all reports were made to the quarter sessions and not to the annual general sessions.

At the beginning of the period under review Lancashire possessed one county asylum, built on the moor above the town of Lancaster. Its accommodation was approximately 480 and it was always full and at times overcrowded. As the population of the county increased, three other asylums had to be built — at Prestwich in 1851, Rainhill in 1853 and

Whittingham in 1873 — all of which had considerable additions made to them in the following years.

From its opening a committee of visiting justices had been appointed annually for the county asylum at the annual general sessions, but this became a committee open to 'all and every' justice of the county who cared to attend its meetings. The Lunatics Act of 1845, however, required a committee of visitors to be elected for every county asylum at a meeting held after 20 December each year. A committee of visitors was therefore elected for Lancaster Asylum, and when other county asylums were built separate committees were appointed yearly for each of them. In 1850 the committee of visitors for Lancaster Asylum became a standing committee of the annual general sessions as did also the committees of visitors of the other county asylums when formed. The members of each of these committees were drawn from all the hundreds, but in each case the justices of the hundred which contained the asylum within its borders had a majority on the committee for that asylum. In each case this majority was divided into groups, each of three justices, and each group performed the legally required duties of visiting for one month at a time. Meetings of the full committees were held monthly.

From 1845 onwards the internal management of asylums was assigned to their committees of visitors who appointed and, if necessary, dismissed all asylum staff, drew up regulations, determined diets and fixed the weekly rates to be charged for the maintenance of patients. They also examined, audited and passed the accounts kept by each asylum treasurer; and were authorised to order all repairs not exceeding £400, to enter into contracts and to control all discharges from the asylum and all transfers to other asylums or workhouses.

On the other hand, the Court of Annual General Session was the legal authority under the Lunacy Acts for all capital expenditure and major repairs. The committees of visitors, too, were required to make yearly reports to the annual general sessions. All asylums were subject to yearly inspection by the commissioners of lunacy after 1842. All plans had to have the approval of these commissioners, while all contracts and estimates required the approval of the home secretary. The consent of the poor law commissioners was also required before harmless patients could be placed in workhouses. The central government was, therefore, a third and potent force in asylum administration.

When the annual general sessions decided in 1839 to adopt the (permissive) County and District Constabulary Act, which empowered them to establish a county constabulary, uncertainty arose about how the affairs of the police should be administered. After experimenting with a constabulary committee consisting of twelve prominent justices and then with one representative of the hundreds, the Constabulary Committee in 1842 was declared an 'open' committee at which any county justice could attend. This met every month in Preston with the result that, for the most part, justices residing in and near Preston attended and ran the affairs of the county constabulary. Growing dissatisfaction with this state of affairs led to a further change in 1860. The justices of each of the seventeen police divisions met yearly, selected one of their number and sent the name to the annual general sessions. These then were automatically appointed, together with eight justices residing in or near Preston who were regarded as representing constabulary headquarters in Preston, as the County Constabulary Committee. As new police divisions were formed additional members were added but no further changes made.

The county constabulary was organised in divisions, each under a police superintendent, and at first these divisions were co-extensive with the petty sessional divisions. As new divisions were formed, however, police divisions eventually included two or more of them. Every month each police superintendent laid his accounts for contingencies and the pay sheet for his division in front of the justices at a petty session court held in his division, where they were examined and signed by two justices. These were then forwarded to the County Constabulary Committee at Preston without reference to the district finance committees of the quarter sessions. The chief constable presented a quarterly report, dealing for the most part with statistics of crime, to each of the four courts of quarter sessions. Occasionally resolutions over police matters were sent from these quarter sessions to the annual general sessions for consideration. The one real power, however, which lay with the courts of quarter sessions in connection with the police was that the general police rate for the administrative county and the local police rates for each police division within the sessions area, as settled by the annual general sessions, were levied at the appropriate court of quarter sessions.

The County Constabulary Committee became a standing committee of the annual general sessions in 1850, and its function was to examine the chief constable's accounts, to authorise payments and, upon his application, to afford him authority in matters of detail. At its monthly meetings much routine business was conducted. From time to time reports on new scales of pay, new police stations or other police requirements were presented for decision to the annual general sessions. When a vacancy occurred in the position of chief constable, the General Finance Committee recommended the salary to be paid, the Constabulary Committee received the applications and drew up a short list, and the new appointment was made by the annual general sessions. All other appointments in the county police force were made by the chief constable, who was in complete operational control of the county constabulary.

The annual general sessions assessed and laid all county police rates and allowed and passed all accounts in connection with the police. It authorised scales of pay and granted gratuities and pensions to members of its force. Its sanction was necessary for expenditure on the building, alteration and improvement of all police stations and contracts connected therewith. Thus in Lancashire at this time the Court of Annual General Session was the undoubted police authority for the administrative county — subject, however, to the general control of the home secretary, whose approval was necessary for rules, scales of pay and additions to the force.

The committees considered so far were all in existence before 1850. After that date, new standing committees were established as the need arose. The first of these was a General Purposes Committee consisting of the chairman of the annual general sessions and six other justices appointed yearly. Its function was to transact all business of a general character not referred to any other committee. In practice nothing of any importance was ever referred to this committee, for, by and large, the annual general sessions itself dealt with all matters of a general character not referred to any committee. The county treasurer and the bridgemasters, who were the only county officials to handle county funds, always had balances in hand and were required to give security in respect of these. The one purpose which the General Purposes Committee ever fulfilled was to check each year that the sureties for these officials were alive and solvent.

In the early fifties the annual general sessions appointed a committee of twelve prominent justices to watch all bills introduced into Parliament in connection with county administration. For some years this committee strove to enlist the justices of other counties in 'a common front' against the threat to the control of their counties. Little enthusiasm was shown for such a project, so the Lancashire Committee abandoned the attempt and, though appointed yearly, became in effect moribund. Then in 1868 the committee was broadened to include all Lancashire peers and Members of Parliament who were county justices, and was constituted a standing committee of the annual general sessions — being styled the Standing Committee to Watch Bills in Parliament, but commonly called 'the Parliamentary Committee'. However, it was one thing to persuade members of both houses of Parliament to accept membership of the committee, and quite another to secure their attendance at meetings and their active interest in its proceedings. The committee again suffered a period of decline, minutes ceased to be kept and parliamentary business involved in securing Lancashire acts of Parliament was entrusted to the General Finance Committee. It was only during the last six years of this period that the Parliamentary Committee really functioned and took a leading part on behalf of the county justices, in first opposing, and then seeking amendments to, the Local Government Act of 1888 before it became law.

Between 1848 and 1869 a dozen acts of Parliament were passed in connection with the diseases of cattle and sheep, and these laws were carried into effect by the courts of quarter sessions, which in Lancashire left their administration to the justices of the petty sessional divisions. When the Contagious Diseases (Animals) Act of 1869 enjoined the appointment of committees to carry out the act and inspectors to enforce its provisions, cattle plague committees were appointed at each of the Lancashire quarter sessions. A similar act was passed in 1878, under which the annual general sessions appointed, as a standing committee, an Executive Cattle Plague Committee for the administrative county, and delegated to it its powers under these acts, except that of levying a rate to defray costs. The committees appointed at the quarter sessions continued to be appointed as local cattle plague committees. Then, at the annual general sessions, all these committees were automatically elected as the Executive Cattle Plague Committee. Superintendents, inspectors and even sergeants of the county police were appointed as inspectors under these acts to keep down expense. No minutes were ever kept but the local committees made reports of a statistical character to the quarter sessions and the executive committee to the annual general sessions.

The repair of roads or highways was, like the repairs of bridges, an ancient common law obligation on all the inhabitants of a county; but, whereas the administrative unit for the repair of bridges was the county or hundred, that for highways was the parish. By the middle of the nineteenth century it became clear that the parish was too small a unit to deal effectively with the highways, and that, with the development of railways and consequent loss of traffic, even the turnpike trustees were no longer financially able to do so. These trusts had been created for terms of years, and after 1850 they expired at a steadily increasing rate. In 1862, therefore, to deal with the first problem an act was passed which empowered justices in quarter sessions to unite several parishes into highway districts consisting of the resident county justices and elected waywardens, one or more for each parish. The second problem was the subject of a provision of the Highways and Locomotives Amendment Act of 1878. It provided that any road that had ceased to be a turnpike since 1870, or any road that might in future cease to be a turnpike, was to become a main road. The highway authorities were to be responsible for the maintenance of as many of these main roads as lay within their respective areas, but half the expense was to be contributed from the county rates. It was found that 379 miles of main roads would be subject to such contributions, but that these dis-turnpiked roads were unevenly distributed over the hundreds. It was therefore decided that the main roads should be hundred and not county roads, and that rates for these should be levied separately on each hundred. Each bridgemaster was appointed surveyor of roads for his division or hundred.[5] The bridges were left for the most part to the quarter sessions and the bridgemasters, but the annual general sessions in 1879 formed a Standing Committee for Highways. This committee, consisting of twenty-four members representing the quarter sessions, met four times per year.

The actual maintenance and repair of the main roads was carried out by the 134 highway authorities in the administrative county and their accounts were audited by the government district auditors, re-examined by the county auditor and

31

allowed by the county's Committee for Highways. The provisional and final orders for the formation of highway districts were made at the quarter sessions but otherwise these courts had nothing to do with the main roads. The surveyors of roads had the twin duties of inspecting and certifying that the roads were in good repair and of checking items in the accounts of the highway authorities. The members of the Committee for Highways resident in each quarter sessions area formed a sub-committee to negotiate with deputations from local and highway authorities. To the County Commitee of Highways was delegated the examination and allowance of accounts and the investigation of claims for contributions. The annual general sessions drew up bylaws for the roads, issued licences for locomotives, laid the rates for roads and took all decisions over main roads.

Other standing committees were formed in order to carry out responsibilities placed upon the county justices by acts of Parliament. Thus, in 1855 a Militia Storehouse Standing Committee was formed; in 1878 a Sale of Food and Drugs Act Committee, and in 1879 a Reformatory and Industrial Schools Committee. They were concerned with administrative details and made yearly reports to the annual general sessions. Lastly, in 1880 the licensing committees formed for each of the courts of quarter sessions were designated as standing committees.

Thus by 1880 the system of delegating administrative duties to standing committees, an implicit feature of local government today, had been introduced and extended to all departments of county administration by the annual general sessions.

With the adoption of agendas for meetings, notices of motions, standing orders and standing committees in 1850, the annual general sessions emerged from its Georgian conception of itself as a special kind of quarter sessions to embark on a course which gradually made it more like a local government council. In the last forty years of its existence as the

county authority for Lancashire it achieved a great deal.
Modern, businesslike methods were developed, not only in
the conduct of its meetings, but also in the handling of the
finances of the county. Between 1838 and 1889 gross expenditure rose five-fold, from £82,907 (1838-9) to £418,307
(1887-8), but for the same years government grants-in-aid of
qualifying expenditure increased only from 13 per cent to
22.1 per cent of gross expenditure, and the valuations of the
administrative county changed only three and one-quarter
times, from £3,721,598 (1841) to £12,219,872 (1884). Yet
the averaged county rate levied in 1887 (4¼d in the £)
differed little from that levied in 1838 (4$\frac{1}{16}$d in the £).
In no other county at this time were county finances so
concentrated under one authority or so closely examined by
both justices and officials as in Lancashire.

During these years a large building programme was also
carried through. Three new county asylums, new county
offices at Preston, new assize courts at Manchester, eight
militia storehouses and 115 new police stations were built.
This capital expenditure totalled £2,868,471, but the net
capital debt of the county in 1889 was only £614,928
because much of the capital expenditure had been financed
out of revenue. A county constabulary was established and
expanded from 352 men in 1840 to 1,321 in 1888; this force
was recognised as one of the most efficient of its time.

With the responsibility for the poor law vested in the
boards of guardians and with the securing of charters of incorporation by some Lancashire towns and the establishment of
local boards by others, the annual general sessions became
clearly more of an intermediate authority than it had been in
the period before 1838. It was also brought into closer contact with the central government. Its prisons, asylums and
police force were all subject to government inspection, a fact
which spurred the justices to make their police efficient, to
bring their institutions up to the standards laid down by
government departments and to improve conditions within

them. With the delegation of functions to standing committees, the annual general sessions became much more of a body concerned with outlining general policy, exercising overall control and giving final authority than it had been earlier in the century. In short, it had come to occupy, in the administration of the administrative county, much the same sort of position that the present county council does.

There was little criticism of county administration after 1850. The change to an elected county council in 1889 was inevitable in accordance with the principle of democratic government, local as well as national, developed in Victorian times.

Notes to this chapter are on page 187

Chapter Two

The Making of the Borough of Salford, 1830-1853

R. L. Greenall

Historically, one of the most interesting features of Salford is
that it has developed as a separate unit from Manchester.
Although the borough was very much a Victorian creation,
apologists for Salford's separate status have always drawn
attention to the fact that it has ancient roots, going back to a
manorial division of the eleventh century.[1] Surprisingly,
perhaps, separation persisted when the two towns entered the
era of rapid urban growth and industrialisation in the late
eighteenth and early nineteenth centuries, although at first it
seemed that it would not. In the local Acts of 1765 and 1776
Manchester and Salford had one body of police (ie street or
improvement) commissioners. In 1792 when a new act was
obtained, the two towns were again treated as one, but from
the very start the commissioners divided and formed two
distinct bodies, one consisting of the commissioners resident
in Manchester and the other of those in Salford. Appointing
separate establishments and levying separate rates, they henceforth confined their activities to their respective towns.

The separation in 1792 was the first manifestation of the
attempt, successfully carried through in the years 1825 to

1832, to establish Salford's claim to a distinct identity, based on the medieval 'manorial borough' status of the township, implying separation from, and equality with, the 'borough' of Manchester. It was quite extra-legal, and remained so until a new Manchester Improvement Act in 1828, the preamble of which acknowledged the *de facto* division. Salford then obtained its own Improvement Act in 1830, and administratively the two towns went their separate ways. The important point is that separation from Manchester came before (though not long before) the period when both towns secured a municipal framework of local government. Except for an abortive attempt to amalgamate the borough of Salford and the city of Manchester in the 1880s, they have remained administratively separate ever since.

The modern borough of Salford was created in 1853 by the uniting of three townships — Salford itself, Broughton and Pendleton. This was the culmination of a process that had started when they were brought together to form a new parliamentary constituency under the Reform Act of 1832. It was, however, one thing for the boundary commissioners, a powerful external force, to cause them to be united for the purpose of electing a Member of Parliament; it was quite another for the local ratepayers to agree to form a mutually acceptable and effective pattern of local government, however badly these rapidly growing districts needed one.

When in 1844 the regime of the police commissioners came to an end, Salford acquired a municipal charter. It was, however, quite unable to persuade its two neighbours to become part of the new borough. Indeed, separatism was so strong that it was not until 1853 that the borough was enlarged to become co-extensive with the parliamentary division, and even then the subsequent union was far from comfortable. The compromises necessary to allay the fears of the Broughton and Pendleton ratepayers resulted in a municipal constitution of singular complexity. The struggles to create a framework of government for these three growing townships,

located at the heart of what contemporaries called 'the manufacturing districts', is the subject of this chapter.

The government of the townships in 1830

In economic function, population size and social structure,
Salford, Pendleton and Broughton were very different in
1830. They remained so until the 1870s, and most of the
problems of local government that were to beset Victorian
Salford stemmed from this simple fact.

By 1831, Salford had grown to be an industrial town of
some 41,000 people. As such it was four times as populous
as both Pendleton and Broughton combined. In contrast to
tightly packed and largely working-class Salford, Broughton,
with a population of only 1,600, was a rural suburb. Its eleva-
tion and location on the north side of the factory districts
made it desirable as a residential area, and as early as 1825
'well-to-do-people fond of rural retreats' were removing across
the Irwell and building their villas on the 'breezy heights'.
Much of Pendleton was also suburban. Along the 'Old Road'
to Eccles there were houses of varying degrees of opulence
ranging from respectable villas to the considerable mansions
of men like Thomas Potter, the cotton merchant, and
Benjamin Heywood, the banker. Until the end of the century
West Pendleton continued to remain a congenial suburb of
Manchester, rivalling Victoria Park and Higher Broughton. On
the other hand, there were industrial settlements in Pendleton
at Douglas Green and Charlestown where workers found
employment at the collieries and in the textile mills. Its population in 1831 was 8,500. The fundamental division between
the three townships was firmly lodged in that most solid of
bases, class differences.

The Webbs noted that: 'the local government of Manchester
was rendered specially complicated and confused by the distribution of obligations and powers among various conflicting
jurisdictions.' This is no less true of Salford. In 1830 these
jurisdictions were three in number. The first, the vestry, was

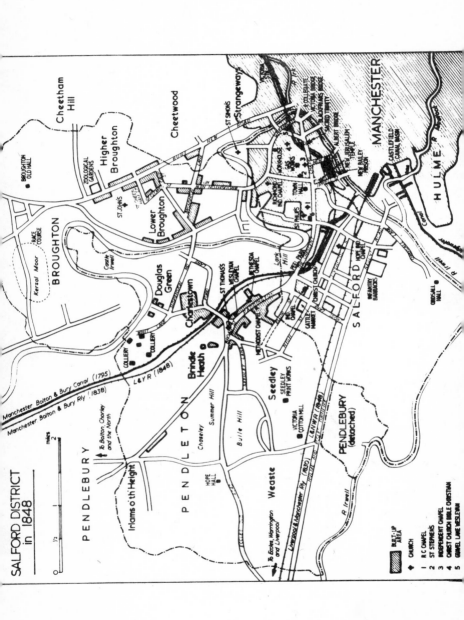

SALFORD DISTRICT in 1848

BROUGHTON

PENDLEBURY

PENDLETON

SALFORD

MANCHESTER

HULME

Cheetham Hill

Cheetwood

Higher Broughton

Lower Broughton

Strangeway

Douglas Green

Charlestown

Brindle Heath

Seedley

Weaste

Irlams o'th'Height

PENDLEBURY (detached)

Kersal Moor

RACE COURSE

ZOOLOGICAL GARDENS

BROUGHTON OLD HALL

HOPE HALL

St.JOHNS

St.SIMONS

ST THOMAS

WESLEYAN CHAPEL

BETHESDA CHAPEL

METHODIST CHAPEL

COLLIERY

COLLIERY

SEEDLEY PRINT WORKS

VICTORIA COTTON MILL

INFANTRY BARRACKS

CHURCH

CASTLE MARKET

CHRIST CHURCH

SACRED TRINITY

COLLEGIATE

VICTORIA BRIDGE

ALBERT BRIDGE

NEW JERUSALEM TEMPLE

NEW BAILEY PRISON

CASTLEFIELD CANAL BASIN

WORKHOUSE

TOWN HALL

St.PHILIPS

Summer Hill

Butte Hill

Charley

Lark Hill

The Park

Castle Irwell

Manchester, Bolton & Bury Canal (1795)

Manchester, Bolton & Bury Rly (1838)

L.& Y.R. (1848)

Liverpool & Manchester Rly. (1830)

ELY.& M.R. (1848)

R Irwell

R Irwell

To Bolton, Chorley and the North

To Eccles, Warrington and Liverpool

miles

0   ½   1   2

BUILT-UP AREA

CHURCH

1   R C CHAPEL
2   ST STEPHENS
3   INDEPENDENT CHAPEL
4   CHRIST CHURCH BIBLE CHRISTIAN
5   GRAVEL LANE WESLEYAN

an element of parish government at which churchwardens, sidesmen, overseers of the poor, and surveyors of highways were appointed; it spent most of its efforts in the administration of poor relief and on the upkeep of the roads. The second was a singular manorial survival, 'the Court Leet, View of Frankpledge and Court of Record of our Sovereign Lord the King for his Hundred or Wapentake of Salford'. The King's steward was the Earl of Sefton, and the Earl's deputy, a barrister, held this court twice a year in Salford. Although it had jurisdiction over certain other townships in the hundred, its main function was to punish perpetrators of nuisances in Salford and to appoint the boroughreeve, two constables and other township officers.

The third element in the township government of Salford was the body of police commissioners. In March 1830, as already noted, a new act, the first to apply solely to Salford, became law. There were to be 120 commissioners, elected by persons assessed for poor and police rates. Under the committees of this body the township was to have its first introduction to continuous and reasonably effective government in the nineteenth century.

But the securing of the 1830 Act was by no means Salford's first move in the direction of becoming a town with an identity and status of its own. In 1825 a committee of citizens acting independently of the commissioners reasserted certain 'old rights' to hold a market in Salford. Although the creation of the modern borough of Salford was largely the work of Radicals and Liberals, the members of the Market Committee which began the process were all Tories. Despite the fact that this antiquarian committee had not succeeded in finding a copy of the original charter (which turned up only in 1835) to substantiate the claim, they were successful in obtaining the right to erect a partly covered market from the Duchy of Lancaster. When it was completed in 1827 this included offices and a hall for the use of the Salford authorities. Eventually the new police commissioners were to purchase the market hall and begin the many extensions of what became (and is still) Salford Town Hall. This period (1825-32) brought the erection of this building, the passing of the Liverpool and Manchester Railway through Salford, the opening of two new churches of the Establishment, the erection of a dispensary and the securing of parliamentary representation. With these events the separate identity of the 'new town' of Salford was firmly established.

By 1830 there was need for a new approach to local government in the township. It was abundantly clear that the powers of the existing forms of government were insufficient to tackle the problems of uncontrolled urban growth. Buildings had sprung up to house people migrating into the town, but there were no building regulations. The narrow ways left to foot and wheeled traffic were often ill paved, uneven and full of holes in which the water and garbage accumulated. There was no effective street cleaning or removal of refuse. There were few sewers or water closets, and few houses had an ashpit or privy. Cowsheds and slaughterhouses were located in main streets, down which periodically the blood ran in streams. At night the streets were ill lit and there was only minimal police surveillance.

The hundred court leet and the vestry lacked the powers needed to tackle these problems. There was uncertainty and confusion over their respective spheres, and there seemed to be no way to combine responsibility with efficiency in these two bodies, who published no accounts and had no regular committee system. The most important officers were selected not by the ratepayers of Salford, but by the Earl of Sefton's packed jury, and these were almost always Tories, who blocked reform. The vestry was too absorbed in the problems of poor relief to give much time to the wider concerns of town government. Both the vestry and the court leet (which met only twice a year) were far too inflexible to meet the growing need for effective town government. In the period 1830 to 1844 their powers were taken over by the police commissioners and by the effects of national legislation, most notably the Poor Law Amendment Act of 1834.

Pendleton and Broughton, neither of which (yet) faced the urban problems of Salford, were governed by means of township officers under the general Lighting and Watching Acts. Neither had a boroughreeve; their senior officers were two constables nominated by the hundred court leet. Both townships at their vestry meetings appointed overseers of the poor, and there were also surveyors of highways. Pendleton, with a larger and also more industrial population, had a somewhat more developed framework of administration than Broughton, although both remained seriously under-governed until 1853. It had a workhouse and a board room where township meetings were held; in Broughton township meetings were held in the Griffin Inn. In both, well-to-do gentlemen filled the voluntary post of constable, with a paid deputy acting as day policeman. With this minimum of government these two townships faced the problems of a growing population, relying on voluntary short-term expedients to cope with individual issues as they came along.

Salford under the police commissioners, 1830-1844

Although by the early 1840s it was becoming clear that the government of Salford needed to be improved and extended, it would be wrong to overlook the very real achievements of the police commissioners in the years 1830-1844. In general their most important reform had been to build an administrative structure where one had scarcely existed before. By 1844 Salford was run by seven strong and virtually autonomous committees, a system which thus had a considerable history before the municipal council came into existence. The commissioners had acquired the market and town hall in 1834, built a large new cattle market in Cross Lane on the west side of the township in 1836, rebuilt the two main bridges over the river into Manchester and acquired a gas works. Salford, emulating Manchester, was an early exponent of the idea of running a municipally controlled public enterprise to provide a high-quality service to the consumer, and using the profits to pay for town improvements. The private gas company had been bought out in 1831, and within five years such was the growth in demand that a virtually new plant had to be constructed. By 1844, Salford had not only been supplying gas for its own needs for nearly thirteen years, but had also been selling it to Pendleton for the last six.

The commissioners had also made a start, albeit a somewhat tardy and reluctant one, in bringing together the night watch and beadles to form a police force, and had, by the prosecution of nuisances and scavenging, made Salford somewhat less insanitary than it had been in 1830.

Yet the achievements of the police commissioners, though real, were limited, and by the standard of later municipal activity very modest indeed. It must, however, be recognised that the financial and political obstacles facing the commissioners were very considerable. The problem of how to develop a framework of town government at a time of rapid urban growth was not one on which governments at Westminster in the 1830s or 1840s gave much lead. Under commissioners such as Salford's there was no break with the past; their method of working was traditional, the plans of local reformers were often limited, and the development of effective local government came only slowly. Financial problems also beset them, though this was not a problem peculiar to Salford. But the Salford finances in the 1830s were administered unskilfully, and the police commissioners were in existence at a time of severe fluctuations in the economy with high unemployment in 1832 and 1838-42. In these years of depression there was widespread poverty and high poor rates, and the capacity of the smaller ratepayers to pay their other local taxes was greatly diminished.

In the first years of the commissioners there had been a good deal of activity; soon, however, it began to tail off. This was because the commissioners were involved in acquiring properties which, although they would in time prove to be profitable, initially involved outlays that were higher than anticipated. Also many of the prominent people who had served in township offices and on the jury of the court leet had been elected police commissioners and were not anxious to see too much power transferred to the new committees of that body. In 1835, however, there was a definite shift of power from the vestry and court leet to the commissioners, the result of which was a noticeable growth in the volume of activity on the part of the Salford authorities.

This process was also part of the change in the balance of political power in Salford. With the coming of the first instalment of parliamentary reform, political activity in the township was very lively. The Reformers succeeded in returning Joseph Brotherton, a local Radical, to Parliament as the first Member for the borough, and he held the seat until his death in 1857. In this period Reformers came to dominate the police commissioners. The struggle for power at first focused on the positions of the boroughreeve and constables. Before 1835 the holders of these posts were invariably Tories, but in that year the Reformers persuaded the Earl of Sefton, who was a Whig peer and had supported the Reform Bill, to stop packing the jury of the hundred court leet with Tories. Thenceforward the three township officers were usually Radicals or Reformers. Their domination of Salford's local politics was destined to last for another thirty years. In the 1830s the Tories made desperate efforts to recover their lost dominance in local affairs, and also to wrest the parliamentary seat from Brotherton, but to no avail. Their only success in these years lay in preventing the amalgamation of Pendleton and Broughton with Salford in the years 1842-4 and in 1847.

In two of Brotherton's electoral campaigns his campaign committee chairman had been William Lockett, a successful silk mercer, who had retired from business in 1831 and devoted himself to local affairs in Salford until his retirement in 1848. He was the leader of the 'Improvers' among the commissioners. More than anyone else, he steered local administrative fortunes in this period. Around Lockett was a group of energetic men, amongst whom William Harvey, Charles Tysoe and Joseph and John Kay were prominent. From 1835 to 1836 these men gradually came to assume leadership on the various committees of the Salford police commissioners. They formed a tight interest group, united by business, family, religious and political relationships.[2] Under their direction administration became energetic again. In 1840, however, a financial crisis came which lasted until the end of 1843. Although Lockett and the Improvers must bear some responsibility for it, they overcame it successfully. When it was settled the final phase of the era of the police commissioners began. It was a time of growing local problems in Salford in which the Improvers, against considerable opposition, brought about the end of the police commissioners by successfully promoting and carrying through a campaign for a municipal charter and a new Improvement Act.

The most serious failures of the police commissioners were in policing and sanitary matters. In the period 1839-41 the Salford ratepayers were thrown into a state of agitation when, following the setting up of the rural police forces, the government brought in a bill that threatened to put the police of all towns without municipal corporations under the county magistrates and county police. In February 1841 Lockett, much to the alarm of the ratepayers, advocated that Salford should petition for a charter, but this prospect temporarily receded when the attorney general ruled that boroughs and towns of over 10,000 people were to be exempt, provided that they policed themselves efficiently. Incorporation did not come to the forefront of Salford politics again until over a year later.

In his *Report on the State of Large Towns in Lancashire* (1845), Dr Lyon Playfair noted that only about one-fifth of the length of sewers, or one-seventh of the number of streets finished in Manchester under a similar Act, had been finished in Salford during the same period. He drily added: 'the Salford Act has not been this inoperative owing to the absence of any necessity for exercising its powers; on the contrary the sewerage of the town is in a most objectionable state.' But, as Playfair recognised, it was not only local inactivity that was responsible for the relative failure in paving and sewering, but also the inadequacies of the 1830 Act in this respect. By 1844 it had become clear to the Improvement Committee that before it could widen the main roads of Salford and step up the rate of paving, sewering and scavenging, it would need to acquire powers that only a new local act could give.

It must also be said that the desire for such an act was much greater than the desire of incorporation. There was no great ambition on the part of the Improvers to enjoy the trappings of a corporation and royal charter. Nonetheless, if one reason for petitioning the Queen for a charter was to secure a better structural framework of government, and another, to expand the municipal borough of Salford to take in Pendleton and Broughton, a third did concern status. Salford was neither borough nor county, and the attitude adopted by the home secretary after the passing of the County Police Act had underlined the disadvantages of Salford's position.

There was also need for a more coherent framework of government. The power of the court leet over the appointment of the township officials was increasingly resented, while the police commissioners were too large and unwieldy a body. As an institution they scarcely encouraged civil pride; they served reluctantly and often absented themselves from meetings. In any case, traditional township meetings, whilst nominally democratic, were in reality a poor method of ensuring effective government. Issues would be crudely raised or opposed by cabals or even individuals claiming to represent ratepayer opinion faithfully, and every step could be, and often was, fought over in semi-anarchic fashion. It came to be

45

felt by the Improver party that a charter establishing a municipal council to which councillors were elected each year would be a more effective way of securing representative local government.

The impending demise of the police commissioners was accompanied by the decline of the other parts of the old pre-1830 structure — the hundred court leet and the vestry. If their extinction was slower and more protracted than the abrupt end of the commissioners in 1844, they were nonetheless on the way out. The court leet had lost control of the police, and (since 1835) of the nomination of boroughreeve and constables. Just as significantly, it was losing its role as the court before which nuisance offenders were presented and fined, the activities of the Scavenging and Nuisance Committees in the township superseding it. Although it continued to meet until October 1867, the last presentment before it occurred in 1858: thereafter its meetings were empty formalities.

The vestry also declined in this period. It had lost control of the beadles, and the New Poor Law took away its principal functions. It managed to keep some importance with regard to the surveyors of highways until 1850, and survived in a vestigial fashion until 1897, though largely without function in the pattern of government.

1844: Incorporation and the new Improvement Act

In late 1842 a petition supporting incorporation was circulated among the ratepayers of the three townships. The original plan to incorporate the whole parliamentary borough was, however, soon thwarted by the rise of partisan township feelings in Pendleton, and later in Broughton. At a meeting of Pendleton ratepayers in January 1843 strong feelings of township autonomy were expressed by the opposition. Pendleton 'would be guilty of suicide if it became tied to Salford in questions of municipal government', a leading Pendleton separatist declared. In a united borough Pendleton councillors

would always be a minority, and would be out-voted by
the representatives of the other townships on Pendleton
matters; the rates would increase steeply to pay for the
more pressing Salford problems; the township would have
to foot the bill for a costly municipal staff; it would be
liable for the cost of the upkeep of the turnpikes at present
borne by the trustees; and, finally, the old Tory argument that
passions would be raised annually by political contests for
municipal office to the detriment of peace and property was
revived. Lockett, heading a deputation from Salford, had little
difficulty in countering most of these points, but (in those
days before the growth of an awareness of the sanitary issue)
he failed entirely to make a convincing case to the Pendleton
ratepayers of the benefits incorporation would bring.

There was also opposition from inside Salford, from the
Tories and Chartists. There was great suspicion of the alleged
secrecy and arrogance of the Improver party. Disquiet was
expressed that the Liberals were embarking on a venture that
had been shown to be unnecessary in March 1841. The
Chartists wanted to be sure that public opinion, or rather
ratepayer opinion, was in favour of incorporation. Lockett
pointed out that all ratepayers had received a copy of the
petition for the charter, and he was able to show subsequently·
that the Incorporators constituted a majority both in numbers
and in size of property. This, however, was true only of
Broughton and Salford; the Pendleton authorities refused the
committee access to the rate books.

The Incorporators had further setbacks in the autumn. The
first was that for the crucial year 1843-4 the jury of the
court leet, breaking the 1835 agreement, elected three of the
most cantankerous Tory upholders of the status quo to the
offices of boroughreeve and constables. Hence in the year in
which the new Improvement Act and a charter were to be
solicited, opponents of the proposals occupied strategic township offices. The other setback was that in the winter of
1843-4 the separatists in Pendleton finally defeated the plan

to extend the charter to that township. It was by then clear that the charter was not going to be extended to Broughton either, despite 'the want of lights and an added protective police' in that township.

The charter of incorporation for the borough of Salford was duly secured on 16 April 1844, but only the township of Salford was brought under the Municipal Corporations Act, where henceforth the inhabitants, through 'the Mayor, Aldermen, and Burgesses', were to be recognised as one body corporate.

Despite the failure to incorporate Pendleton and Broughton, it was nevertheless a notable achievement for Lockett and his supporters. They had secured incorporation without incurring the ratepayers in any expense, and the transfer of power from the commissioners was not accompanied by the furore that Manchester had experienced after 1838. However, the first municipal election was yet to come, and it was to be an embittered affair because it was the culmination not only of the struggle for incorporation, but of another movement, which had run parallel to it, and which was an infinitely greater source of discord — the agitation for a new Improvement Act.

At the end of January 1844, when Lockett introduced the draft of a street widening bill to a suspicious meeting, there was again opposition from the Tory/Chartist coalition. They feared a new act on the grounds of cost, on whether its provisions would be fully available for scrutiny, and on the issue of consultation. Suspicion of the Improvers went deep. The Chartists threw themselves energetically into organising opposition, and soon other objections were raised. Fear was expressed that the bill would give the authorities too much power over buying out property owners. It was questioned whether Salford could afford it, and in the debate the financial crisis of 1840-2 became a central issue. It was argued that the township had not got enough property to mortgage to pay off interest on the £25,000 that would have to be borrowed and that the ratepayers would have to pay higher rates in the end. The Chartists disliked a clause that had been inserted in the bill allowing the outgoing boroughreeve and constables to nominate their successors to the court leet, and a prominent Chartist accused the Improvers of being 'a greedy grasping junto, like those in Spain. Some twenty of them kept all the power in their own hands'.

In the face of this opposition the Improvers withdrew the bill and replaced it with an amended one. Subsequently much anger was generated between the two sides over whether or not the second bill was merely an amended version of the first, or a totally new one. Meanwhile the promoters of the bill had not been idle. Petitions in favour were sent to Westminster from the board of guardians, the overseers of the poor, the surveyors of highways, and local doctors and clergy. Four-fifths of the commissioners petitioned in favour of it, and a general petition from the ratepayers was organised.

The parliamentary committee was due to begin its hearing on Friday, 3 May 1844 and Lockett, John Kay and Tysoe went to London as a deputation to promote the bill in committee. To their intense anger they found the borough-reeve and constables already there with legal advisers, re-questing papers and surveys to be laid before the committee. In the event, however, the committee stage of the bill was a triumph for Lockett and the Improvers; the bill was passed without further delay, receiving the Royal Assent on 6 June.

The background to the first municipal election in Salford was an intensification of the war of words, between the boroughreeve and his supporters, and Lockett and his Improver 'junto'.[3] But the electors preferred Lockett and the Reformers, returning seventeen of them to six Tories and one Chartist. The poll was high, with about 75 per cent of the burgesses voting.

In the last week of July the council met for the first time. Eight aldermen, all Liberals, were elected from outside the ranks of the twenty-four councillors, and Lockett became the first mayor of Salford. With regard to the offices of borough-reeve and constables, the new Improvement Act stipulated that the name of the mayor and four others should be submitted to the court leet; the election of the first three of them to the township offices was to be a formality. Henceforward the court had no choice but to accept this arrangement.

Salford under the municipal council, 1844-1853

The Liberal victory in the first municipal election meant that the business élite was represented on the local authority in a way that it had never been before, or for that matter was ever to be again. Eighteen out of the thirty-two aldermen and councillors were merchants or manufacturers engaged in one or other branches of the textile industry. Another seven were former businessmen, now of sufficient private means to be listed as 'gentlemen'. 'Small men' — retailers, licensees and the like — who normally played a big part in nineteenth-century local government were in a tiny minority. Perhaps because of this municipal Salford got off to a good start. Leadership in this first period of the council's history was given by the men who had pushed through incorporation and the Improvement Act in 1844. Lockett, Harvey, Kay and Tysoe all became aldermen. Lockett served a second term as mayor, Kay succeeded him, and Harvey served two terms in 1857-9. For more than two decades after 1844 the political complexion of the Salford Council remained Liberal, and the Tories had to live with their minority status. After the administrative experiences of the period 1840-3, the new council sensibly employed a well paid town clerk and borough treasurer, and the Watch Committee took the important step of appointing a chief constable. The number of committees of the council grew from the seven inherited from the police commissioners in 1844 to twelve by 1853. This framework of authority worked well, and it is hard to disagree with Sidney Webb's impression of this period of local government in Salford: 'a somewhat energetic council going on vigorously with paving, putting down smoke and nuisances, and developing its gas and water, and parks and library and gallery'.[4]

The expansion of the gas concern was increased greatly after 1844. A contract with the Broughton gas inspectors was signed in 1846, and in 1851 pipes were run into Pendlebury to supply that township with gas as well. Between 1834 and 1851 the output of the works had been increased from 200,000 to 80 million cubic feet. For the period 1840-52 profits amounted to £73,500, of which some £16,500 was spent on the two enlargements to the plant while £44,000 was paid over to the Improvement Committee and the Finance Committee.

In 1845 a large house with seven acres of ground standing on the western side of the township was purchased by the association recently set up to provide Manchester with public parks. Although the actual purchase of Peel Park cost the Salford ratepayers nothing, the council took over the running of it from the start. It was the finest of the new Manchester parks and soon became immensely popular. In 1850 its amenities were greatly extended when the house was converted into a museum and free library. Salford was one of the very first towns to provide these services, and the idea of free libraries was quickly taken up by other towns such as Liverpool and Manchester.[5]

The municipal council was very prompt in initiating a programme of street improvement under the terms of the 1844 Act. In three years the Improvement Committee, with the help of a loan sanctioned by the act, had initiated works which cost £38,000. These included the widening of Chapel Street, the main thoroughfare of Salford, and the building of a new bridge across the river Irwell. This burst of street improvement, badly needed for some years, was an achievement, but at the rate industry, commerce and traffic was growing in the 1840s it is not surprising that by 1850 further street improvements were necessary. These were, however, difficult to carry through. The powers of borrowing and compulsory purchase granted to the council by the 1844 Act had been exhausted and improvements could only be effected with the consent of the owners of property. It became clear that before more could be undertaken a further local act would have to be obtained.

From 1845, increasing information about the problem of insanitary urban conditions began to stimulate interest in public health for the first time in Salford. There was urgent need for action. In the opinion of Engels, Salford in 1844 was dirtier than Manchester. There, at least, he declared, 'they try to clean out the filthiest corners of these Augean Stables. Nothing of this ever seems to happen in Salford. I am sure that the narrow side streets and courts of Chapel Street, Greengate and Gravel Lane have never once been cleaned since they were built.' He was probably quite correct in this allegation, as, under the commissioners, scavenging had largely ignored the alleys and courts and had concentrated on the main streets. The result was that Salford in 1842-5 had an average death rate of 30.9 per 1,000, a figure considerably over the national average for 1844 of 21.6 per 1,000 persons. Salford was unhealthier than Pendleton, which had a death rate of 24.5, while middle-class Broughton, with a death rate of 16.3, was as healthy as most suburban and rural districts in the country. Dr Playfair pointed out in 1845 that in Salford the average age at death was 20 years 8 months, which was the lowest in all Lancashire with the exception of Liverpool. The average age of all who died over the age of twenty was 49 years 6 months. He concluded: 'There must be something radically wrong in a community, when the artisan reaches only 15 years of age, and has 28 years less chance of life than the gentleman from the day of birth or 11 years less of adult life.'

It is clear that before the council could begin to take positive steps to improve sanitary conditions, three preliminary conditions would have to be fulfilled: (i) that the authorities become aware that Salford was insanitary, but could be made healthier by public action; (ii) that it was recognised that existing Acts of 1830 and 1844 did not grant the local powers necessary to make this possible; and (iii) that, as a consequence, new local acts granting these powers would have to be secured. The years 1844-50 saw the first steps towards the fulfilment of these conditions. A Paving and Soughing Committee was formed in addition to the Improvement Committee, and the Scavenging and Nuisance Committees were spurred into more vigorous action than hitherto. In 1850 a new local act, which was the equivalent of the 1848 Public Health Act, was secured. It greatly extended the sanitary and street improvement powers of the corporation, with clauses regulating the use of gas profits for the purposes of improvement, and ensured Salford a better supply of water than hitherto, as part of the great Manchester Corporation Waterworks Scheme.

The uniting of the three townships in 1853
By 1852 it had become clear that the need for sanitary reform in Broughton and in particular in Pendleton could no longer be ignored by the ratepayers of those two townships. The choice that faced them was either to have local boards of health under the 1848 Public Health Act, or to follow the action advocated by the Salford Council and the General Board of Health in London, and amalgamate with Salford in an enlarged municipal borough.

Amalgamation in 1853 was a case of third time lucky. The first abortive attempt to amalgamate the three for municipal purposes had been made, as we have seen, at the time of the Salford incorporation in 1844. The second had been in 1847, when the original moves had actually come from a group of Broughton ratepayers. Their proposal was effectively sabotaged by another Broughton group acting from deep suspicions of Salford's motives. Relationships between the districts were left extremely fragile.

In the twenty years since 1830 the population living in Broughton and Pendleton had more than doubled to 7,000 and 14,000 respectively, and yet the two townships remained virtually without local government, being serviced from outside with regard to police, lighting and gas. In the face of the growing concern with sanitary matters it was felt by some ratepayers that this situation could not go on.

In 1850 and 1851 Robert Rawlinson, a superintending inspector of the General Board of Health in London, had, in response to petitions from the ratepayers, visited and reported on their sanitary state. The reports endorsed those who said that Pendleton and Broughton could not act independently of Salford in matters of sanitary improvement. Broughton, he pointed out, was a wealthy and salubrious suburban district of Manchester and Salford. Unlike Salford or Pendleton, there were 'no masses of people congregated together in crowded and ill-ventilated dwellings, half clothed, poorly fed, and worse housed'. Yet, despite its being healthy, Rawlinson emphasised that there was need for a public body in Broughton to promote sanitary reform. The population was likely to continue to increase. Although no ill effects had yet been felt, there were sanitary defects which, if small at present, required active attention if trouble was to be avoided in the future. The time had come, he felt, when 'the construction of private (ie house) drains should not remain a matter of choice'. There were also cesspool and water problems, and much of the private sanitary efforts in Broughton in the last twenty years had been wasted. He concluded his report by recommending the setting up of a local board of health in the township, and expressing the hope that it would co-operate with Salford and Manchester in the very large task that all this involved. When he turned to Pendleton, Rawlinson graphically described a rapidly growing industrial township almost totally unregulated as to construction or sanitary arrangement. It was therefore no surprise that the death rate was higher than Rawlinson thought reasonable, and that the population was vulnerable to epidemic diseases that were, in a large measure, preventable by sanitary improvements.

Those who wanted an amalgamation of Broughton with Salford may have been disappointed that Rawlinson had not been more specific about this in his Broughton report, in which he wrote about the Manchester area in general terms only. They could not complain about his recommendations with regard to this question in his Pendleton report a year later. He suggested an 'extension of boundary, so as to include Pendleton and Broughton within the municipal borough of Salford, as they are within the parliamentary borough'.

It was Brotherton, the Member of Parliament for Salford, who took the initiative in bringing the townships together. In December 1851 and January 1852 he met the Pendleton and Broughton authorities and put proposals to them for the union of the three townships. Aware of the sensitivity of feelings in the townships, he proposed an intricate federal arrangement. This was agreed to, and it was then taken to the special committee of Salford Council, which also agreed to it. Having been approved of by the authorities of all three places, public meetings of the inhabitants of Broughton and Pendleton were called to consider the proposition.

The matter facing the out-townships was whether it would be advantageous to remain separate from Salford and adopt the Public Health Act (with its overtones of 'London management'), or to go beyond that and agree to become part of the enlarged municipal borough. After Rawlinson's report, there was little difficulty in settling for the latter in the case of Pendleton, where sanitation had overcome separatism. At first things also went smoothly with regard to the attitude of the Broughton ratepayers. In March 1852 a joint meeting of the three committees was held in Salford Town Hall and a draft of the bill was read and agreed to. A request to Parliament to suspend standing orders so that a bill might be introduced right away was, however, turned down and so the bill did not have its first reading until the autumn. But it did not meet any serious opposition until early in the following year.

The first sign of trouble came in February 1853 when the abstract of the new bill was published in the press and it was revealed that Salford would supply both out-townships with water. This evidently was not to the liking of certain Broughton ratepayers and the Manchester Corporation, which since 1850 had supplied Salford. It was observed shortly after, in the *Manchester Guardian*, that though the bill proposed that Salford was to supply Broughton with water, 'it seems that Broughton wants to deal with Manchester', and that an agreement had been swiftly reached and that 'the inhabitants of Broughton may expect ere long to have a water supply in quantity adequate to their needs'. This was the first serious move by the opponents of amalgamation to arrive at their own solution to the problem of Broughton's future. Manchester joined the Broughton opponents (and two railway companies) in opposing the bill before the Select Committee of the House of Commons, and there followed a series of acrimonious exchanges between Manchester and Salford Councils. However, this water problem was settled outside the committee.

In Parliament the bill had a smooth passage in the Commons, was given a first and second reading in the Lords, and was then referred to a special committee under the chairmanship of the Earl of Lucan. It was at this stage that serious opposition came from the same group of Broughton Tory ratepayers that had opposed incorporation in 1847. The arguments of their counsel somewhat confused the committee of the House of Lords, though in the end it decided to pass the bill with two escape clauses. Clause 67 stated that the act was not to extend to Broughton unless more than one-third of the number of inhabitant householders, rated to an amount exceeding half of the whole rate of the township, had given

their assent before 1 August 1854 at the latest; and Clause 68
that this information would have to be certified by two
justices of the peace. The bill was then sent back to the
Commons, who approved the amendments as a fair test of
whether ratepayer opinion was for or against union with
Salford.

The final obstacle to legislative action was removed when,
at Westminster, the Broughton petitioners and the town clerk
of Salford reached agreement regarding the arrangements for
amalgamation. Salford was conciliatory on the details and
agreed to pay the parliamentary costs of the Broughton
petitioners. The bill became law on 14 June.

The two safeguard clauses might have seemed to a reasonable observer to go more than half-way to meet the fears of
Broughton ratepayers that Salford was not going to 'annex'
them, and make them foot its bill. Nevertheless the deal was
regarded by some of the die-hard separatists as a sell-out, and
a cabal led by James Bancroft, a Manchester alderman who
lived in Broughton, continued to campaign vigorously against
the bill.

Everything depended on whether or not the ratepayers of
Broughton would indicate their support for or against the bill
under clauses 67 and 68. A vigorous Committee for
Incorporation was set up, supported by a number of
prominent Broughton residents, to oppose Bancroft's party.
They campaigned in the summer of 1853, their differences
being speedily converted into feuds. Eventually, on 27 July,
a petition for incorporation was put before two magistrates as
required by the act, and they accepted that owners of property amounting to more than one-half of the total assessment
for Broughton had shown that they were for it. The act therefore became operative in November 1853.

If the opponents to amalgamation were bitterly disappointed by the passing of the act they had no need to be,
because the separate identities of the two out-townships were
anything but submerged. The administrative structure that

was created by the Salford Extension and Improvement Act of 1853 was an intricate federal arrangement. It was described in 1862 in these words: 'Salford is . . . divided into three districts; each district has its separate management, its separate staff, its separate estimates, its separate rates (and by no means at the same proportion in the pound), its separate borrowing powers, and its separate property, which is not to be liable for the debts of the other districts. Each district is, in fact, an *imperium in imperio*, the Corporation merely consisting of the representatives of the several districts. In fact the borough has been designated "A Trinity without Unity".' [6]

As Brotherton had proposed in 1851, the council was to consist of a mayor, eight aldermen and forty-eight councillors elected by the burgesses of eight wards (four in Salford as before, and two each in Pendleton and Broughton). Administration of the borough was to be carried out under five general committees, whilst 'improvement' functions, i.e. the making, paving, draining, cleansing and maintenance of the streets, were to be handled by three sets of district committees.

Decent Liberal compromise though it was, the 1853 arrangement created almost as many problems as it solved. Broughton remained unassimilated into the borough. Given the social differences and the separatist feelings of the districts, this was perhaps inevitable. But the 'borough' and 'districts' arrangements made improved government difficult, though not impossible. Finances were rendered extremely complicated; interdistrict jealousies over financial, gas and water matters were virtually built-in; and it may be doubted whether the sanitary improvement of the whole area, a prime reason for incorporation in Rawlinson's reports, was well served by these continuing divisions. In a town which was growing ever more industrialised, populous and crowded, this complex administrative framework was a drawback. Yet these arrangements continued without serious modification until 1891.

Notes to this chapter are on pages 187-8

Chapter Three

Baptists & the Working Classes in Mid-Victorian Lancashire

J. Lea

The size of the Baptist denomination in mid-Victorian
Lancashire defies any but the roughest estimation, as it is
often difficult to identify those subject to its influence.
Statistics published in the annual reports of the local Baptist
Association[1] recorded only registered church members, and
contemporaries recognised that of their congregations only
about one-third were in membership.[2] This would mean that
by the 1880s probably some 56,000 people worshipped
regularly in Lancashire Baptist chapels. Even so there were
many others subject to Baptist teaching. The churches organised missions, which often became independent chapels and
which in poor areas could have a permanent and lasting effect.
Between 1843 and 1887 there were never fewer than thirty-
eight active missions in any one year, and in eleven years
there were over sixty. Those attending such places cannot but
be counted among the Baptists, for even if their religion was
not regularised, the denomination was at least one constructive factor in their lives.

Similarly, Sunday schools increased Baptist numbers. It
was held that many pupils were, if not church members,

practising Christians. With five years as the average period of attendance at the Cloughfold schools, through which four thousand pupils passed in the fifty years after 1825, and with about a third of the Accrington population attending the Blackburn Road Chapel school between 1843 and 1871, such claims would not appear to have been unfounded.

Furthermore, especially in the second half of the century when once-a-day attendance at chapel was a growing complaint, irregular worshippers were not negligible, for from such people W. P. Lockhart was to build up a church of over seven hundred members in Liverpool. When all factors are considered, therefore, the influence of the Baptist churches was extensive, reaching probably about a hundred thousand persons in Lancashire by the eighties. Much of this impact upon the region was not formalised — as the Methodists jibed, Baptists were 'good marksmen, but they do not bag the game'.

Within these ill defined denominational ranks were representatives of all social strata below the aristocracy.[3] They included members of the upper middle class, 'men of large pecuniary resources', exemplified by William Snape of Darwen, who provided hospitality for Lord Hartington during the 1885 general election campaign. Chiefly however, congregations were drawn from the lower middle class. It was something of a local denominational boast in 1850 that 'Those to whom God has given neither poverty nor riches, are the men, who . . . constitute the large majority in Christian churches,' and Beatrice Webb described the Baptists of Bacup as a 'charmed circle of artisan and small bourgeois life'.

But for all this, working men were not unknown among Lancashire Baptists. Church histories, denominational journals, official reports and records all reveal that many congregations were working class in character. This was true, for example, of certain churches in Accrington, Brierfield, Blackburn, Church, Clowbridge, Coniston, Dalton, Liverpool, Oswaldtwistle, Padiham, St Helens and Deerplay. Similarly, chapels established by subsidy or benefaction in deprived districts were attended by the poor, and missions, such as those in Manchester at Ancoats, Wilmot Street, Upper Medlock Street, Elm Street and Homer Street, in Liverpool at Byrom Street, William Moult Street and Westmoreland Street, in Preston at Dock Street, in Bacup at Millgate and in Accrington at Royds Street, were organised for people living in slums.

But working-class Baptists were not confined to specific chapels in particular places. They were also to be found in the prosperous churches attended by the rich. The pastoral visitations of H. S. Brown, pastor at the affluent Myrtle Street Chapel in Liverpool, took him to the homes of Baptists 'in many a dark alley and dingy court . . . in which crowds of poor wretches are crammed into small and filthy rooms'. In fact surviving church records show that it was customary for churches to devote the collections taken at communion services to the poor in the congregations.

Above all else, however, it was through the Sunday schools that Baptists reached the working classes. The 'utter ignorance and the stolid indifference . . . of a large number of children' was regarded as the greatest difficulty teachers faced 'in the most populated districts'. Minute books of Sunday school teachers' meetings in, for example, Accrington, Manchester and Bacup, narrate perpetual confrontation with all the problems of social deprivation from illiteracy and disorder to stench. Whilst in recent studies of Victorian religion, therefore, it has been denied that the churches maintained close contact with the working classes, the situation in Lancashire Baptist chapels would seem to indicate that this conclusion requires qualification. It was quite common for working-class people to support the denomination in the county, though they were never in a majority and were chiefly attenders rather than members at the chapels; and equally some of John Bright's 'residuum' or 'sunken sixth' were present in Baptist chapels, missions and schools.[4]

Consideration of working-class presence among Baptists

must go beyond this however. The situation was never static. Within the chapels there was considerable social interchange. Regional economic progress and the educational advantages of affiliation with a church could bring personal success. James Barlow, orphaned when nine years old and earning one shilling for every chair he repaired, became in time 'one of the makers of Accrington' and the town's second mayor. Naturally it was achievements of such a man as this that were readily recorded, yet fall in social standing was also common. The minutes of church meetings reveal that not only were elaborate, discreet procedures of inquiry established to examine cases of bankruptcy, but that these procedures were frequently invoked, suggesting Baptists could become impoverished as well as prosperous.

In between these two extremes others rose and fell less dramatically in the social scale, if for no other reason than that all were subject to the economic fluctuations of the period. In 1842, the Lumb church was all but closed because new local industries, having removed the demand for domestic manufacture, themselves failed to maintain production. With the renewed slump of 1847, the county Baptist Association recorded that 'all have felt the pressure of the times in a greater or less degree', and a year later that 'mercantile embarrassment and want of employ' was still being experienced by the churches. Again in 1858, an unfavourable economic situation caused the cancellation of chapel building appeals at a time when the closure of a local mill threw out of work 'nearly all the scholars and congregation' at the Millgate mission school. Similarly, the post-1870 depression caused difficulties. From 1878 the churches began to endure 'hard times — unremunerative trade and lessened wages', with Baptist congregations in Wigan, Dalton and Haslingden suffering particularly, through unemployment in the coal, iron and cotton industries. Again, depression intensified from 1884, causing further migration in search of work and making always some members of the Bacup churches unemployed.

The consequence for individual Baptists of economic instability was most clearly indicated by the suffering endured during the Cotton Famine. In December 1862 9,508 people connected with the denomination were without work, and in February 1863 sixty churches were distributing relief amongst their congregations. Circumstances were so bad that some pastors could not be paid stipends, and some 'of our people, who have been comparatively well-to-do, are now on the verge of want'. At Ogden Baptists emigrated, and at Sabden some entered the workhouse. Elsewhere, one family of six received 5s a week, and another of seven but 4s. In a small church twenty were in desperate need, with ten more 'obtaining a bare subsistence'. For some, distress was lessened by the 1s 6d received weekly from the parish, for others by the 9d per day earned breaking stones for roads.

Manifestly the economic standing of people within the churches fluctuated constantly, with all in danger of social frustration. If some emerged from poverty to obtain respectability and perhaps more, others teetered on or over the brink of want, and all at some time experienced, either directly or indirectly, the hardships of working-class conditions.

This characteristic of the churches was consolidated by the fact that in their secular employment most Baptists were closely identified with the regional process of industrialisation. In 1852 it was claimed that congregations were 'for the most part operatives, or persons engaged in manufactures', and significantly, apart from Inskip in the Fylde and Tottlebank in Furness, there were no rural chapels. Baptist communities were part of the economic and social revolution of the day. Employers and professional men among them were manufacturers in textile, chemical, mining and metal industries, or commercial magnates in shipping, accountancy, banking, wholesale and retail trade. Artisan Baptists included those responsible for industrial plant (foremen and overlookers), men with technical skills (block-printers, cabinetmakers, joiners, painters, stonemasons, spinners, weavers, loom-tacklers), clerical staff and shopkeepers. Unskilled labourers in Baptist ranks were employed as coal and iron miners, railway navvies, bobbin-winders, tierers and cloggers; there was even a pedlar and a dry-waller. The majority of Baptists thus depended upon industry and its ancillaries for employment, so that working-class life was intimately known and experienced by those attending the churches.

The intellectual climate of the chapels showed this to be the case. Educational attainment was as precarious as economic viability. For all but the wealthy, it was derived from the teaching provided by the churches, mainly in Sunday schools. The result was that the literacy of the majority was merely functional, leaving them 'limited in their reading to the Bible and the hymn-book, the Magazines and the Circular Letter, the Pilgrim's Progress and the Saint's Rest'. Frequently the intellectual limitations of the laity obtruded: H. S. Brown once had to explain the meaning of the word 'locality' which he had used in a sermon; Joseph Hanson, authoritative in an Accrington church, was without formal schooling, while John Hudson of Burnley 'had plenty of work placed upon him' because he was educated above average. At Farnworth, John Isaac, a trustee of the new chapel, was semi-literate.

Against this background of educational deficiency, the Education Act of 1870 could not but have a beneficial effect. By 1877 it was being said, 'To many . . . it seems superfluous now to go to God's House for *instruction*.' But the main impact of rising educational standards still lay in the future. In the mid-nineteenth century, few Baptists exceeded the inadequate education of the working classes generally.

The question therefore arises as to why these particular churches should be successful in attracting people from the lower social classes. Part of the answer must be that, in the multiplicity of religious ideals which they set before their congregations, they offered a purposeful way of life. Firstly, the highest moral codes were demanded; secondly, private devotions were imperative, and thirdly, attendance at all church services, especially on a Sunday, was enforced. Indeed sabbatarianism was strict — with some people, even Saturday evening was regarded as an integral part of the following day and devoted to meditative preparation. Fourthly, Baptists were encouraged to support financially their chapels and denomination. At Ebenezer Chapel, Bacup, in addition to the pew rents that always provided the stipend, 'each member who is able [is] expected to contribute two pence per week towards the support of this place'. Denominational bodies, such as the Baptist Missionary Society and the County Home Mission, organised annual collections and subscription schemes that drew even upon the farthings of Sunday school children. Fifthly, local charities were upheld as being worthy of help. In Liverpool, H. S. Brown could always raise in his church whatever he required for relief work, 'and that not in large sums from one or two wealthy friends, but in many sums of various amounts down to the widow's mite'.

Finally, the aspect of personal devotion which all who attended Baptist services were most expected to fulfil was individual involvement in the churches' evangelism. Everyone had 'a special work and position in the church, peculiarly his own', and all could discharge their responsibilities by 'lay preaching, Sunday and Ragged School teaching, tract distribution, cottage meetings and visiting'.

So fundamental was this concentration on lay evangelisation that it became institutionalised, in the Lay Preachers' Society adopted by the county Baptist Association in 1883. By 1887 there were 240 lay preachers in 110 churches. Indicative of the reality of the laymen's contribution to the denomination's evangelism was the circular letter devoted to the subject in the 1873 Annual Report. It specifically noted the career of Jonathan Hargreaves, and thereby recognised a work that all social classes could undertake. Hargreaves began life in such destitution that he could not attend Sunday school until his employer provided him with boy's clothing. In time, through membership of the Sabden church, he became an intense lay evangelist, 'the weeping preacher', in the district around Padiham and Billington, until in 1854 a new church at Waterfoot grew out of his work, calling him to be its first pastor in 1860. When he died nearly twenty years later, Hargreaves left a congregation that had grown sevenfold, a new chapel building that was free of debt, and a reputation that was respected by all denominations. Such success was the pinnacle of religious achievement with regard to the ideals set before the laity. It demonstrates what the churches expected from their supporters.

Manifestly this was idealistic. The real situation among Baptists was different. Churches could be 'the very nests of discord and the arenas of the bitterest hate'. So far short did conduct fall of requirements that even at the local Baptist Association's Jubilee the moderator saw fit to devote his address to 'The Necessity of Harmony'. Instead of humility he found among Baptists self-righteousness; instead of fellowship, snobbery; instead of sympathy, back-biting; instead of doctrine, criticism; instead of co-operation, fault-finding; instead of evangelism, apathy; instead of friendliness, formalism. He concluded: 'It would take no less than an angel from heaven to satisfy everyone's wish, and even then . . . someone would find fault with the shape of his wings.'

There would even appear to have been some sexual immorality in the churches, as six people were excluded for this offence from Leeming Street Church, Preston, in the twelve months after July 1848, and four from Ebenezer Chapel, Haslingden, in the ten months after July 1863. Obviously, therefore, cant and an hypocrisy that rested content with lip-service existed, which did nothing to make the denomination attractive, even as its harsh discipline of members was also thought to prejudice outsiders.

Yet for all this, the importance of the ideals upheld must not be ignored. The denomination's distinctive rite of adult baptism by total immersion encouraged sincerity. Some were attracted by the exclusiveness it implied; others found the experience intimidating; yet whatever their reaction, those attending Baptist chapels accepted believers' baptism out of conviction. Consequently, for the committed, to be devout in all the churches sought to do was to realise the ultimate purpose in life. For the less committed, there was at least a sense of contributing to progress, because to contemporaries religion was making world-wide civilising advances, and talk of the millennium was common. For the indifferent church life provided, at the lowest level, friendship, a club, entertainment and something constructive to do. But over all else, because of the piety demanded, the churches clothed those associated with them in respectability, at a time when respectability alone could mean social survival. In the words of one who attended the Huncoat Church throughout the period, 'the plain old sanctuary, 32 feet by 27 inside [had] kept him straight, [though daily] in contact with rude and wicked men' Chapels provided a purpose in life and with that purpose 'character'.[5]

Chapels had more tangible benefits to give than this, however. At a time when social services were provided only by organisations of co-operative self-help, churches were important social centres. They gave the means as well as a way of life. Clothing (Dorcas) societies were common, helping in the provision of bedding, furnishings, suits and dresses, either by supervising a fund of regular savings or by holding sewing classes. Provident societies were to be found almost everywhere for, as the Rev Charles Kirtland of Sabden explained, 'the majority of our brethren are able to do no more than provide for their present wants'; they were involved by periods of recession in distress from which they could never recover; they were embittered in sickness by the loss of income and by the threat of a death which would leave dependants without provision, even to defray funeral costs; and they were soured as old age approached under the shadow of the workhouse.

In an attempt to ameliorate the plight of so many, Kirtland

published an actuarial benefit scheme, applicable to workers with wages between 30s and 10s per week. According to subscriptions, between 2s and £3 per week was provided in sickness, from £1 to £30 at death, and from 2s to £1 per week in retirement. Such systems of self-help 'on the principle of mutual assistance' were widely adopted – five hundred people contributed to the fund at Ebenezer Chapel, Bacup, in 1869.

Chapels also made extensive cultural provision. In a measure this was a product of attentive participation in church services, but Sunday schools played a very real part, too. The educational importance of these institutions in a generation of voluntaryism is not hard to imagine. Significantly, according to the records of teachers' meetings at the Ebenezer Sunday School, Bacup, between 1865 and 1871, the ages of the pupils ranged from ten to thirty-two years, with the majority aged from seventeen to twenty-two. In a period before a national education system emerged, the explanation of this situation is to be found in the pursuit of literacy by those who had not obtained it outside the chapels.

Yet the cultural provision of Sunday schools went beyond elementary schooling. They also encouraged recreation, by the organisation of day trips on the rare holidays. Many had lending libraries – a thousand volumes were available for borrowing at Astley Bridge in Bolton in 1859, and during 1874 250 people made use of the 2,515 books at Church. Most schools organised a Young Men's Mutual Improvement Society too, established (in something of a stock phrase) 'to promote the religious, moral and intellectual improvement of its members'.

Also attached to Sunday schools were Bands of Hope, which were not merely temperance organisations; for to counteract the fascinations of the drinking and singing saloons they arranged musical entertainments. Indeed, there was a strong musical tradition within the Lancashire churches, from the bucolic Rossendale 'sings' to the professionalism of

W. H. Jude at Myrtle Street Chapel, Liverpool, and this was undoubtedly part of the cultural climate created.

Overriding all else, however, in the social benefits the chapels brought to the poor was the presence of wealth. Men of substance served two functions. In times of need they provided relief; in normal times they provided both the business experience and the financial credit necessary to administer the large sums of money collected by denominational and welfare bodies. Both functions of the rich were demonstrated in the Cotton Famine. As the crisis intensified in 1862, the local Baptist Association created The Lancashire Baptist Relief Fund, administered by a committee of businessmen whose credibility attracted subscriptions from throughout the country, raising in all nearly £7,000. This the committee distributed among the churches, but it also organised the collection and delivery of tons of aid in kind, the creation of temporary schools, and help for special cases of difficulty. Here was proof indeed that the rich served to enhance the welfare facilities the churches made available to all connected with them. Through the variety of the benefits they provided in a *laissez-faire* society, the chapels became effective social centres around which the needy gathered in search of security.

Because there were many representatives of the working classes in the churches, and because the churches consciously catered for working-class needs, the political attitudes of Lancashire Baptists could not escape from the social problems of the day. The denomination did not encourage working-class agitation, however. There were three reasons for this. Firstly, in days when most people worked more than fifty-six hours per week, the heavy religious demands made by Baptists left the working class faithful with little time, few resources and small energy to be expended upon other matters. For them church life and activities absorbed all available leisure. Beatrice Webb found that the working men in Bacup Baptist chapels took 'little interest in politics . . . their thoughts are set on getting on in this world and the next'. They had no time for anything else.

Secondly, secular working-class activity was impeded by a strong apolitical tradition in the denomination. To a degree this was the result of historical circumstance, the older generation having grown up when Nonconformists were excluded from public office. But even after the repeal of the Test and Corporation Acts, cultural, economic and religious prejudice continued to discriminate against dissent, perpetuating an attitude of passive citizenship. Furthermore, if the law of the land bred political indifference, so did the structure of Baptist churches. Because they were voluntary organisations, no activity could be undertaken that would alienate any part of the congregation, so that neutrality was the only viable public posture. The local Baptist Association repeatedly asserted that it was 'purely religious', warning pastors to 'avoid all interference with civil matters'. Leading ministers needed no such guidance. James Lister and C. M. Birrell in Liverpool, Joseph Harbottle in Accrington and Alexander McLaren in Manchester all publicly refused to participate in political affairs; and even in the 1880s, when this attitude had begun to change, W. P. Lockhart, happy to appear on political platforms, refused to refer to political questions in the pulpit. Even if the apolitical tradition declined, it was never to be eclipsed.

Thirdly, the working classes were restrained by the patriarchal nature of the churches. Given the remorseless pressure of demands made upon the laity, the educational and economic inadequacies of the churches and the voluntary character of the denomination, it was inevitable that the influence of the wealthy should predominate. In fact, Baptists enjoying prosperity, intelligence and position were expected to use their advantages to the benefit of all, a responsibility recognised in the office of deacon. Although poor men became deacons by dint of their piety, office-bearers were mostly men of substance. Forming a governing court, they set the tone, so that if any breach were to be attempted in the defences of apolitical neutrality, it was inevitable in whose interests the assault would be made. As long as working people sought to draw upon the benefits chapels afforded, their submission before the middle classes was unavoidable.

These three factors operated together to produce a general suspicion among Lancashire Baptists of all working-class movements. The suspicion was variously demonstrated. The violence so closely associated with mass movements alienated them as social obedience was a facet of Baptist religion. Similarly, sabbatarianism separated the churches from the mass of the people. With Sunday the only time of relaxation for so many, most working-class organisations functioned on that solitary free day. To Baptists this was both a desecration of the Sabbath and a distraction from church worship and work.

But what frustrated Baptist participation in local working class agitation most was ultimately nothing more than misgiving about 'the masses' themselves. They were seen as infidel, if not hostile to religion, and said by their ignorance, vice and godlessness to be 'sapping the very foundation of public order, happiness and security'. The churches existed to rescue their congregations from, not embroil them with, the mass of the people. This was of course self-righteous, but in the context of the brutality and degradation of Victorian urban life, it was not without some justification.

Yet the fears aroused went beyond this. Working-class irreligion was held to be impregnated with socialism, and socialism was interpreted as synonymous with aggressive atheism. This was not as extreme as it first appears. In the forties and fifties atheist socialist missionaries were working regularly in Lancashire, as part of a national 'Atheist Mission' which made marked progress in Manchester, Liverpool and Accrington. The effect of their lecture campaigns was felt particularly among Baptists, for Emma Martin, a former editor of the *Baptist Magazine*, had lost her faith and joined the crusaders.[6] Prejudiced, therefore, by an ignorance that confused atheism with socialism, and by a suspicion that they were a prime objective of special attacks in a general atheist campaign, Lancashire Baptists tended out of hand to dismiss as dangerous any working-class movement influenced by these forces.

With such deep-rooted suspicion of the proletariat, it was inevitable that Baptist involvement in working-class agitation should be minimal and unrepresentative. The Ten Hours Movement elicited little response. Short time committees frequently presented the double disincentive of meeting in public houses on Sundays. Furthermore, by 1838 the movement was already tainted with violence.

It was true however that, as the campaign moved towards its eventual success, some Dissenters did appear as 'new and rare supporters', and in this belated development a few Lancashire Baptists contributed. At Bolton they had stood apart from the opposition of other nonconformists throughout, from 1830 under the leadership of Rev William Fraser, and from 1842 under that of his successor, Rev James Fyfe, on the grounds that: 'the present system of working long hours . . . retards the progress of moral cultivation which is essential to the welfare of the rising generation.' Elsewhere support was more tardy, not emerging at Oldham until 1844, at Preston and Padiham until 1845, and at Bacup until 1849. For the rest, the majority gave neither encouragement nor discouragement, and if they tended to be apathetic they were mostly indifferent to a campaign that was little more than a distraction to their congregations.

Baptist attitudes towards Chartism were similar, but more antagonistic. Once again the irreligion of the socialist mob was a decisive consideration, but in a county subjected to anti-Poor Law riots before the Charter was taken up, to preparation for armed revolt in 1839, to the use of troops in 1842 and to further insurrection in 1848, it was the physical force element in Chartism that overshadowed all else.

Within the fear that thus gripped Lancashire generally, the Baptists had their own apprehensions, for they had experienced the disruption Chartists could cause. The imprisonment of William Jackson, a member of a Manchester church, for incitement to riot and promotion of rebellion was the negation of all for which they stood. In 1839 at Ashton-under-Lyne a new church had to struggle to survive 'in the midst of a highly excited population', and at Stalybridge, 'through intense political excitement, [the mission] received a severe shock, many of its members having forsaken the purity of their religious profession'. But the chaos brought to the Huncoat church shaped the Baptist response most of all. There, Archibald McPhail, the pastor, unreservedly and with effect, committed himself to the Chartist cause in the Accrington area using the chapel for his political meetings, and so disrupting regular church life that the building was closed for worship from 1844 to 1851. The costs that the fellowship had to bear for litigation to regain its own property proved overwhelming, and the church was eventually saved from extinction only by the generosity of three benefactors. Within the experience of Lancashire Baptists, religion and Chartism were incompatible; the work of their churches was disrupted by Chartist influence and they would have no part in it.

Trade unions met with little sympathy too, principally because the Baptists were themselves divided by the antagonisms between employers and employees. In the repercussions of the 1853 Preston strike, Charles Williams attempted to calm the troubled industrial waters of Accrington, adopting the neutral public position that there ought to be a fairer distribution of wealth; that nothing was done to protect the working people; and that 'strikes were wasteful, mischievous and, even when successful, were not worth as much as they cost'. But the high feeling in the town overwhelmed his attempt to play the arbitrator; he could do no more than obviate the effects of mob violence, and his own congregations were depleted during the period of unrest.

What shaped opinion in Baptist churches was the presence of employers who, involved in disturbed industrial relations, expressed themselves against organised labour. Hence an editorial in the *Manchester Examiner and Times* on 23 February 1867, written by a former local pastor, Henry Dunkley, was unqualified in its condemnation of trade unions. Similarly, S. B. Jackson, a Liverpool merchant, thought the General Cotton Strike of 1878 'stupid' because employers' interests were damaged through the opportunities presented to foreign competitors. Emotions generated in the world of employment percolated through into the chapels, where masters exercising control through donations and the diaconate shaped Baptist attitudes to trade unions.

It would appear, however, that this reflects only one aspect of the situation. If the interests of working-class members were suppressed by the influence of employers, those interests were nevertheless discussed in private. Certainly a debate on the Co-operative Movement in a Bacup Young Men's Mutual Improvement Society would warrant this conclusion. Although again employer-employee relations were in question and co-operation as a system savoured of secularism and atheism, the young men of Bacup saw the Co-operative Movement as 'a mighty level for elevating the working population'. While the advantages of their position allowed Baptist masters to dominate the attitude of Lancashire churches towards working-class activities, working-class members of those same churches, though less articulate and with less effect, still maintained their own opinions beneath the official surface.

None the less, Baptist opinion in Lancashire was chiefly hostile towards working-class radicalism. Yet the way in which the churches organised their chapels and affiliated societies demonstrated both an awareness of 'the condition of the people question' and a desire to resolve it. If they rejected solutions proposed by the working classes themselves, Baptists nevertheless had an acute social conscience, which in time evolved its own brand of radicalism, demanding legislative intervention on behalf of the people, but without socialist centralisation and mass democracy. It was a concientious response to mid-Victorian conditions that progressively developed this attitude.

The Baptists of Lancashire believed that their religion contained two cures for society's ills. The first was the regenerative power of their gospel. With them it became a truism, intelligible only in the context of successful Victorian churches, that the evangelical experience of conversion, saving both soul and body, was the ultimate solution to social problems, and this conviction was not only implicit in contemporary thinking, but was often explicitly stated. Charles Williams of Accrington warned, 'Young man, if you have no spiritual religion in your heart, you . . . are in danger. Only faith in a loving God can save you from overthrow on the battlefield of life.' Alexander McLaren, reviewing fifty years in the ministry, asserted: 'I have been so convinced that I was serving all the varied social, economical and . . . political interests that are dear to me by preaching what I conceived to be Gospel of Jesus Christ that I have limited myself to that work.' The pragmatic H. S. Brown of Liverpool argued that the gospel 'has revolutionised humanity wherever it has gone', and W. P. Lockhart, having witnessed the change — socially, intellectually and culturally — his converts underwent, contradicted the embryonic socialism in John Clifford's paper, 'The Christian Concept of Society', read to the Baptist Union in 1891: 'The masses could never be raised by securing them eight hours' work and a full day's pay, or by providing them with better houses; but by bringing them to Christ, that they might be made new creatures in him.' For Baptists, to be evangelistic evangelicals was to improve society.

The second aspect of Baptist religion, which was thought to advance social amelioration, was the emphasis upon charity. Philanthropy was ubiquitous. It was even one of the motives for the support of free trade. The Corn Laws were to be repealed to provide steady employment and regular supplies of cheap food, and indirect taxes were to be replaced by a permanent income tax; for, as J. R. Jeffery of Liverpool told a select committee in 1852, this was a direct levy on wealth and not a hidden imposition on the needy.

Humanitarianism also inspired numerous Baptists to co-operate in schemes of social improvement. In Burnley Thomas Booth and William Wood founded the local Mechanics' Institute; in Liverpool H. S. Brown used his church magazine, *Plain Talk*, to support Plimsoll's campaign, to demand better housing and to condemn sweated labour; while first James Lister and later Josiah Jones acted as secretary to the Seamen's Friend Society. At Edgeside the Baptist Church took the initiative in bringing gas and water to the town; at Bacup Thomas Dawson assisted the Lee Commission of the Board of Health in its attempt to provide sanitation for the community in 1849, and thirty years later the Ebenezer Chapel contributed to a local relief fund set up during a spate of industrial unrest. In Preston Fishergate Church supported the local dispensary and infirmary; in Manchester Francis Tucker campaigned for better working conditions for shop assistants; Henry Dunkley sought to make hospital charities effective among the needy and Peter Spence used his scientific knowledge to minimise pollution.[7] Examples of Baptist support for such ventures were all but endless, but even so, private acts of charity overshadowed all else. Reference can only be made to outstanding personalities in this regard — George Foster of Sabden, Joseph Harbottle and James Barlow of Accrington, John Cropper, Nathaniel Caine and John Houghton in Liverpool, William Birch, F. W. Crossley in Manchester and James Shanks in St Helens. These were giants of personal generosity in a denomination exhaustively engaged in remorseless philanthropy. While the spread of the gospel gradually reformed society, charity met immediate needs.

Here then was concern for working people. Yet it was doomed to failure, for Baptists had in reality little to offer to stem the tide of working-class distress. On the one hand, the growing numbers of unbelievers, particularly in Lancashire, where church attendance was the lowest in the country, undermined their case; on the other, the social evils arising from a local concentration of population twice the national average, from rapid industrialisation and urbanisation and from the influx of Irish paupers outstripped all voluntary attempts to better society. Whilst they continued always to evangelise and to contribute relentlessly to charity, mid-Victorian Baptists realised this was not enough. In vain did John Bright assure them at the Baptist Association's Jubilee that social progress had been marked in the second half of the century. Some years before the associated churches had already agreed that voluntary good works were inadequate.

As this realisation dawned, changes in the local political scene occurred facilitating the formation of a new approach to working-class needs. Administrative power passed to the provinces. In the first place with the repeal of the paper tax in 1855, the local press flourished. Secondly, in 1865, 1869 and 1885 the parliamentary representation of Lancashire dramatically increased. Thirdly, local governments acquired greater strength. The Municipal Corporations Act of 1835 effected a provincial revolution, replacing the old self-perpetuating Tory oligarchies with new councils drawing upon those emancipated by the repeal of the Test and Corporation Acts.

Furthermore, the possibilities of this situation were perpetuated. The break-up of centralised parties after 1846 frustrated the proposed Trevelyan-Northcote reforms of 1854, leaving the initiative for improvements with local authorities, especially when the Board of Health was abolished in 1858. In 1859 the Rating of Tenements Act extended the local government electorate, giving to the classes from which dissenters were drawn a direct interest in municipal administration. Power in domestic affairs came to be exercised locally, as the permissive legislation of mid-Victorian years acknowledged.

Lancashire Baptists exploited the possibilities of this situation, turning from their apolitical tradition not least because here, amongst other considerations, were further opportunities for their philanthropy. They used local newspapers to disseminate their convictions. Rev Henry Dunkley became the editor of the *Manchester Examiner and Times*; William Snape founded the *Darwen News*; and Rev Charles Williams wrote editorials in the *Accrington Guardian*, launched by Enoch Bowker, one of his congregation. Symptomatic of growing interest in parliamentary politics was the election, at Scarborough in 1880, of W. S. Caine, the first Lancashire Baptist to enter the Commons.

In local government, so many Baptists became active that three illustrations to a general trend must here suffice. At Bolton, where Robert Smalley was councillor and alderman for nearly twenty years, Richard Stockdale was mayor from 1864 to 1866. At Darwen, William Snape served on the local board for six years from 1859, returning to public life in 1874 as chairman of a committee formed to deal with a fever epidemic. Subsequently he presided over a permanent organisation created to superintend local public health, and in this capacity led the successful campaign for the incorporation of the borough, becoming its first mayor in 1878, and negotiating two major Over Darwen Improvement Acts. In Liverpool J. R. Jeffrey, as chairman of the Improvement Committee in 1853, initiated nine public health projects costing a total of three million pounds, led a constant campaign to reduce the mortality rate in the town, and forced the Health Committee to face the problem of overcrowded dwellings and the need for new housing.

As voluntaryism failed to meet the social needs of their day, therefore, Baptists welcomed new opportunities presented to them, and began to support their religious activities by civic enterprise. Such a development involved a reorientation of the denomination's political attitudes, which required time to evolve and become accepted. Experience in the temperance movement served as a catalyst to this process. For Baptists strong drink was doubly pernicious, because drunkenness both had debilitating physiological effects and frustrated the spread of religion. Accordingly, temperance work was an intrinsic part of chapel life almost everywhere. Significantly, as a testimonial to the effort expended in this direction, local associated Baptist churches received a congratulatory memorial from the Lancashire and Cheshire Band of Hope in 1884. To campaign for temperance was, therefore, a major aspect of Baptist social concern. The failure of that campaign, with no reduction in the sale of alcoholic drinks claimed until 1885, could only have far-reaching consequences. It demonstrated, in the issue upon which most Baptist energy was spent, the futility of voluntaryism as a medium of reform; and the appeal to legislative intervention to save an otherwise lost cause established a precedent for other forms of social change. These lessons were moreover reinforced because they were learned in circumstances of controversy over total abstinence as opposed to temperance. In large measure this was a conflict of generations, with the older Baptists advocating no more than moderation, and the younger ones, total abstinence. The differences were real, none the less, even interrupting meetings of the regional Baptist Association, which in 1871 appealed in vain for unity between two sides, each accusing the other of being either 'over-righteous' or polluted with the accursed thing, according to their position. Not until 1882 did the Association find a compromise formula, when it deplored the evils of intemperance and welcomed the work of the Baptist Abstinence Association, but gave it no authorisation as a denominational body.

Divided opinion was the background to the appeal for temperance legislation, and made all aware of the implication of what was being done. It was not until 1863 that the churches first decided to petition Parliament to invoke the powers of the state to support their voluntary work. Sunday closing, the reform demanded, was one that united all sides. Total abstainers made some progress; temperance men moderated the excesses of weekend drinking. In 1871 the Lancashire and Cheshire Baptist Association, careful to emphasise 'the duty of the churches to use all moral means to prevent drunkenness', added a general reduction in opening hours to Sunday closing. In 1872 a call was made for local option, and by 1877 earlier scruples had been so eroded that associated churches expressed themselves 'profoundly convinced that more stringent legislation in reference to the traffic in . . . liquors is needed'. Gradually, parliamentary enactment had become an integral part of Baptist attempts to improve social conditions.

Through involvement in the temperance movement, the Baptists of mid-Victorian Lancashire had arrived at a position to which their working-class membership, their philanthropy, their social conscientiousness and their interest in local government had been driving them. Because in the thirties and forties working-class movements had been identified with violence, socialism, secularism and atheism, the churches had eschewed demands for reform by Parliament. By the seventies, during the relative prosperity and tranquillity of the 'High Noon of Victorianism', they came to accept principles once repudiated. What is important to note is that the transformation was explicable from their own experience as a religious body; it was the pragmatic evolution of their own ideals in new circumstances, and not a response to radicalism in the secular world. For the Baptists, moral reformation remained the key to temporal advance, even if that reformation might now be encouraged by legislation.

And so with time, the Lancashire churches shifted their ground, moving towards popular radicalism — but not socialism. The political thought of earlier generations made that impossible. Instead, the Baptists became involved in the new liberalism that succeeded the Manchester School, enunciated the principles later expressed in Chamberlain's *Radical Programme*, and in the early twentieth century made two Baptists, Tom Glover and Samuel Woods, the first Labour representatives for St Helens and Wigan respectively. The platform upon which W. S. Caine, the first member of a Lancashire church to contest a parliamentary seat, fought his Liverpool by-election in 1873 revealed the direction in which the denomination was moving. Although an employer, Caine was closely identified with the working classes, and he asserted: 'The right of the working-men to sell their labour in the best market must be fully maintained, and I am entirely opposed to any law which treats employers and employed in a different way . . . I will vote for the repeal of all unjust and oppressive penal legislation relating to Trades Unions.'

Similarly, a letter from Thomas Wright of Manchester to the editor of *The Freeman* in 1874, while doubting the practicability of 'Direct Labour Representation', insisted that Baptist support should be shown only for Liberals 'who clearly comprehend all questions affecting working-men'. Even Henry Dunkley changed his attitude criticising, in a series of letters in 1877, the existing law relating to Employers' Liability, on the grounds that it provided no protection for workers.

In the Barrow election of 1886, Caine affirmed: 'It is the duty of Parliament to address itself to the consideration of our poor, and secure a fair livelihood, a freedom from want, a decent home, and other comforts for the poor people of our country.' That these sentiments were shared throughout the Baptist body in Lancashire was demonstrated in 1887. Alexander McLaren, in the Association's Jubilee sermon, anticipated a future when 'the principles of the gospel will be applied in society', with competition restrained and the fruits of industry fairly shared. Lancashire Baptists had moved from suspicion and fear of the working classes to sympathy and co-operation, and as such they came to occupy a political no-man's-land between liberalism and working-class radicalism.

Baptist chapels in mid-Victorian Lancashire were attended by members of the working class; they provided for working-class needs and eventually acted politically in working-class interests. An accommodation between the churches and the lower social orders was achieved. Furthermore, it must be stressed that this was done despite so much that should have alienated working people. The exclusiveness of adult baptism, the self-righteousness of evangelicalism, the formalism of sabbatarianism, the hypocrisy of moral strictures, the preponderance of the middle class, the divisiveness of dress and pew rents, the condemnation of secular radicalism, the bitterness of disestablishmentarianism, the support of educational obstructionism, the opposition to jingoism and the use of the law to change social customs — all were facets of Baptist life that denied the churches popular appeal. Yet to a degree this was overcome. Granted, Baptists did not win universal approval. Nevertheless, the measure of success they achieved in winning working-class support suggests that the findings of some recent research on the period need revising. The separation between the churches and the working classes in Victorian England was not as complete as is often assumed. The chapel was one place where rich and poor could, and did, meet and work together.

Notes to this chapter are on page 188

Chapter Four

Furness Newspapers in Mid-Victorian England

P. J. Lucas

In mid-Victorian England the importance of the press was recognised. F. Knight Hunt saw it as 'a great teacher and an all-powerful instrument of modern civilisation'; Alexander Andrews, not long after the repeal of the stamp duty, declared that 'hundreds of thousands have been added to the number who look to it as a necessary of their existence', while James Grant in 1872 said that 'our existing provincial journals exercise a mighty power over the public mind in the various localities in which they are published . . .'[1]

Politicians, too, recognised that importance. True, there were those who dismissed a newspaper as 'a mercantile speculation and nothing else' and as 'an ephemeris — an insect of the day — which, having performed all its functions, in a few hours disappears'. Others, who were ultimately successful in the struggle to repeal the taxes on knowledge, believed in the educational value of cheap newspapers, and were said to prefer, as a memorial of existing civilisation, a complete file of *The Times*. They regarded newspapers, even cheap newspapers, as 'admirably and intelligently conducted'. Cobden and Bright shared a close interest in the press, and in 1864

Edward Baines, MP for Leeds, grounded a speech in favour of an extension of the franchise mainly on the great and growing circulation of newspapers as conclusive evidence of the increasing intelligence of the masses. An entry in the diary of a Clitheroe weaver on receipt of the *Carlisle Journal* reveals how important newspapers could be to a working man: 'I was very glad to get it. It is the first news I have had from Carlisle this many a month and it is full of news . . . I read it all through, advertisements and all, I was so keen of it.'

Yet when the social historian seeks some assessment of the importance and activities of the press, more particularly the provincial press, after the 1850s he finds little in the textbooks. There are references to the newspapers' struggle for liberty, to the publications of the eighteenth and early nineteenth centuries, to the repeal of the advertisement, stamp and paper duties and, later, to the *Daily Mail* period, and throughout to *The Times*. Rarely will reference be made to provincial newspapers, and even more rarely to those in the smaller towns. Urban histories — with notable exceptions — give but scant attention to the local press.

Among the reasons that may be adduced for this state of affairs is the difficulty of determining the exact influence of the press, and the sheer bulk of the newspapers. Whatever the reason, the provincial press after 1850 seems to have been discounted.

Society is more than just a network of economic, social and political arrangements in which the key figures are few in number and the lines are simple and direct. It is also a process of learning and communication, in which a far larger number of people are involved, so that a variety of interacting levels and overlapping circles of activity may be envisaged. Asa Briggs has said that only by examining particular segments can we understand Victorian England. This chapter briefly examines one such segment — the local newspaper press in the Furness district of Lancashire — in order to indicate something of the importance of district newspapers in Victorian Lancashire and their worth as subjects of study.

Furness in the third quarter of the nineteenth century has been chosen because selection is inevitable when numbers present so formidable a problem and because it is distinctive or representative in several significant ways. Thus, even though the focus is comparatively narrow, important inferences may still be drawn. The industrial importance of the district and the rapid growth of provincial newspapers after 1850 coincided; the locality contained both industrial and agricultural communities; it was an area of much immigration from various parts of the British Isles; it witnessed the birth of the new iron and steel and shipbuilding town of Barrow — a talking point among contemporaries in Lancashire and beyond; much of its population belonged to the working classes at a time when the condition of those classes was improving, economically and politically, and finally, after the middle of the century, improved communications brought the district more fully into the mainstream of English life and ended its isolation. Moreover, small weekly papers were in a real sense more intimate offspring than regional and national ones.

This chapter will look at some of the characteristics of newspapers and newspapermen, and will examine various aspects of the multi-purpose social role those newspapers performed: that of preacher, critic, propagandist, mediator, political partisan and educator, and advertiser.

The Furness press had a modest beginning, but it did not lack variety and vigour. Between 1846 and 1880 twenty-one newspapers were founded. Neither Barrow nor its smaller and much older neighbour, Ulverston, could be dismissed as newspaper centres.[2] Hunt claimed that the prevalence or scarcity of newspapers was a sort of social index. Where there were many journals, he wrote, 'the people have power, intelligence and wealth: where Journals are few, then many are in reality mere slaves'. That this was but a very crude index, even a slight study of Furness, or presumably anywhere else in Lancashire, would reveal; but that the papers were necessary could not be denied.

The qualities that local journals, proprietors and editors should have if they were to be successful were made clear by a correspondent who informed the *Ulverston Advertiser* that

> the essentials of a local newspaper are Parliamentary and market intelligence; foreign, metropolitan, colonial, provincial and general news; railway and shipping ditto; arrivals and departures of trains, steamers etc; a few sensible remarks on the most important and interesting topics of the day; advertisements; an occasional squib and cracker to catch the superficial eye; local and district information; an abstinence from all vulgarity and squabbling with contemporaries; and last, though not least, the old maid's column — births, marriages, deaths.

However, particular qualities were emphasised. In the early 1870s the *Printers' Register* said of one paper that its success was due to a very rare combination of causes: 'There is manifestly the capital, capacity and perseverance requisite to secure the highest measure of prosperity.'

With the experience of the nineteenth century behind him, one journalist, having said that the weekly journal proprietor should have the 'necessary capital, coupled with energy and business aptitude', continued:

> It is essential, however, that he make it first and foremost a paper for the district, devoting a large amount of space to domestic news, and if possible giving some attention to local history and antiquities. But to be a success it must not be conducted on cheeseparing lines. It ought to have a competent staff, and if it can secure as editor a gentleman who takes an interest in county history and antiquities so much the better. However, he must receive such remuneration as will make it worth his while to stay, because the longer he remains in the district the more he will get to know of its people, its history,

and its annals, and his services will, in consequence, become more valuable.[3]

Those Furness newspapers which had but brief lives shared several or all of the following characteristics: birth during an economically difficult year; the absence of men of good calibre; the unwillingness of their proprietors to run them at a loss for any length of time; insufficient local news; and failure to be in any way superior to the established opposition. Amongst the immense number of local newspapers founded throughout the country between 1855 and 1870 there was and continued to be a high mortality.

The uncertainty and expense explains the caution with which a newspaper might be started. Stephen Soulby, printer, stationer, and inventor of the 'Ulverstonian' printing machine (which was still working in many places towards the end of the century) produced his *Ulverston Advertiser* in October 1847, first as a monthly, then for sixteen issues as a fortnightly, before it became a small weekly paper on 10 August 1848. Likewise the *St Helens Intelligencer,* which became a weekly on 29 December 1855, was started as a monthly 'until we find ourselves wanted oftener'.

Failing newspapers might be closed in haste. If William Alsop struggled for a long time to maintain his *Whitehaven News* as a biweekly, he stopped his *Ulverston Times* after only five issues in 1864, just as another Whitehaven man, Edward M'Vea, had done the previous year with his *Ulverston Star.* District newspaper proprietors were usually general printers as well, and much, perhaps most, of their time was devoted to job printing. It was, perhaps, the success of this side of their enterprises that kept the newspapers going.

Increasing expense was reflected in the ownership and staffing of provincial newspapers. Most continued until the 1880s as 'independent single enterprises, though on a middle-class rather than, as earlier, on a craftsman scale'.[4] Contemporaries, of course, were aware of the changes. Grant said

that, whereas the small provincial papers of the mid-1840s
retained no regular reporter,

> now there is no provincial paper of any reputation or influence
> that has not only its sub-editor, but at least one competent
> reporter; while all our great provincial papers have regularly
> retained and well-paid reporters as an essential portion of their
> literary staff.

In an account of the *Preston Guardian* of 1873, it was said
that half a century previously newspapers had been commonly the property of some printer who, though respectable, yet
ranked only with the better class tradesmen. Times had
changed. The proprietor of a first-class provincial paper
was now, by intelligence, education and social position,
essentially a gentleman. In 1869 the *Ulverston Mirror* published an article headed 'The March of Journalism', in which
the writer commented upon newspaper changes. Ulverston's
press, he said, had 'advanced with immense strides from an
insignificant and puny sheet to a couple of healthy-looking
newspapers'. He had before him the first Furness paper, the
Indicator. This had four pages, 'but the matter contained in
them would comfortably come into half a dozen of our
columns'. There was reason for pride. No reader of the
Furness press, or of papers published elsewhere in Lancashire
or England, can fail to be impressed with those issues con-
taining an immense amount of information, much of it fresh
and local (some admittedly the product of 'scissors and
paste' and of suppliers), vigorous leading articles and correspondence columns, and accurate and neat printing. Donald
Read has shown how non-technical innovations, leading
articles and meetings reports transformed the English provincial press from the 1790s.[5] These were the most important
editorial features of provincial papers throughout the nineteenth century, although at district level the generous supply
of local information of all kinds was equally important.

Not all Furness newspapermen were important, but the

district had its representatives who were worthy of comparison with others elsewhere in Lancashire, and, indeed, in England: there was no lack of newspapermen with the vital spark. In 1873 the *Vulcan*, published by Joseph Richardson, founder of newspapers in Middlesborough and Kendal as well as in Barrow, drew attention to an advertisement for an editor of a Lancashire journal. The successful candidate, it was stated, would be a good paragraphist and capable of writing leading articles, taking a verbatim report, and reading proofs. *Vulcan* pointed to another aspect of the job when it asked why the advertisement had not added 'and do a little preaching'. Newspapermen of the time were often outspoken and passionate, and gave a local flavour to their papers. Richardson and Bernard Augustus Dromgoole of St Helens were good examples of this type, as was Joseph Alexis Bernard, editor of the *Ulverston Mirror,* of whom it has been said 'He was frequently threatened with actions and sometimes served with writs — but he was not to be coerced. Social and official position was nothing to him; if an abuse existed, he attacked it, and generally with success'. Outspokeness possibly reflected and no doubt contributed to the riskiness of journalistic ventures.

Journalists could be talented, energetic, and public-spirited men. Hunt wrote in 1850 that among country journals were many of great talent and integrity, while Grant wrote that a considerable number of the newspapers in Lancashire were highly respectable and well run. Some newspapermen had a sound printing and/or reporting background; others owed their success and reputation at least in part to their outstanding literary ability, and were first and foremost historians, antiquarians, authors or poets. Lancashire examples include W. A. Abraham and J. G. Shaw, of the *Blackburn Times*, and William Hall Burnett, editor of the *Middlesbrough News*, then the *Blackburn Standard*, and latterly managing editor of the *Blackburn Express*. The fame as poet of John Stanyan Bigg, editor of the *Downshire Protestant* and of the *Ulverston Advertiser*, earned him recognition in the *Dictionary of National Biography*, while Richardson was responsible for the production of histories of Furness and Cleveland. It was the poetry as well as the journalism of Francis Leach, editor of the *Barrow, Furness and North-Western Daily Times*, which was subjected to savage criticism.

Whatever their intellectual interests, many provincial editors and proprietors took an active part in the lives of their towns and districts. Shaw was the first head of a Preston school because of his great interest in the problems of the deaf and dumb; Abraham was a magistrate; Dromgoole was an improvement commissioner at the time he launched his *St Helens Weekly News*; George Carruthers, a leading Barrow journalist who had worked for the *Preston Guardian, Bradford Observer* and *Lincoln Standard,* was an active participant in municipal affairs as well as a commentator upon them; and the inspiration behind the *Barrow Daily Times* was the town's leading man, James Ramsden, managing director of the Furness Railway Company.

Provincial newspapers were in one sense the product of general forces. They can be explained in terms of the repeal of the advertisement duty in 1853, the compulsory stamp in 1855 and the paper duty in 1861; by the sharing to some extent of rising national wealth after about 1850 by all members of society; by easier communications; and by the growing and increasingly literate population. In another sense, newspapers were responses to particular needs and this illustrates the vitality of the press. The *Barrow Herald* was born relatively early in the town's history, in 1863, to serve local interests — all those affected by the capitalist group; the *Barrow Daily Times* was inspired, in the boom years of the early seventies, by the need to advertise a new town and thereby to attract investments and labour and to win orders; the *Barrow Pilot* was the product, presumably, of the energetic Carruthers's proprietorial ambitions, while the *Vulcan* drew its energy from hostility to both Ramsden and (initially) Richardson, who felt the former had betrayed him over a business agreement. The *Ulverston Advertiser* was needed as the local supplier of local news; as Furness developed so the papers of Kendal and of Lancaster could be dispensed with. The *Ulverston Mirror* was a response to the need for outspokenness against those who wanted things to remain as they were and to the need for a platform for liberalism. In other places, too, politics was the midwife. Common features included independent discussion of local and general matters and impartial and full reporting of local events.

It has been suggested that the strongest argument for a free press is curiosity on the part of the community about public men and affairs in order to 'censure or applaud'. *Vulcan*, in particular, held that the conduct of public men was a fair field for comment, and in its pages there appeared regularly savage attacks on individuals in prose, verse and cartoon. As 'a flagellator if not unmaker of councils, a projector of schemes, and a man fired with local patriotism by the town he had adopted', Joseph Richardson taught Barrovians 'to qualify and modify their respect for the high and mighty, and they appreciated it'. The newspapers emphasised that they were 'representative', that is to say they were written for, and used and read by, all social classes, a point very generally made, and perhaps significant at this period of a 'viable class society', in which the social classes had learned to coexist.[6] Moreover, in a masculine society newspapers were read and used by women, including working-class women. Dromgoole's *St Helens Newspaper* even had contributions in dialect, common to many newspapers, written, nominally at least, by a woman, 'Sayroh Lankyshur'.

Newspapers could be, and were, used as a platform from which the discontented could attack the authorities, often in the most outspoken way. If it is fair to say that 'the new cooperative societies and the new trade unions enabled thousands of ordinary people to understand and to apply the principles of democratic control', it may be equally fair to argue that progress towards democracy was helped by the fact that the newspapers provided a means by which those who had reason to do so could attack 'Authority', especially the 'Authority' immediate to them. They also gave an opportunity for people to express themselves in public. As de Tocqueville remarked, 'Newspapers become more necessary in proportion as men become equal.' Thus a very high percentage of letters to the Furness press were critical of councillors and magistrates. In *The Age of Equipoise,* W. L. Burn notes the importance of 'the cantankerous man, the man determined to air a grievance, public or private . . . the almost professional exposer of "jobs" or abuses'. Robert Loxham, grocer and councillor, was a good example of this kind of man. The following are the headlines over three of his letters to Carruthers's *Pilot*:

> 'Alleged illegal sale of corporation property'
> 'Alleged illegal sale of land'
> 'Alleged illegal refunding of registrar's fees'.

In 1875 Loxham concentrated upon streets and sewage, distributing letters to the *Barrow Herald, Barrow Pilot,* and *Barrow Times.* As a retail shopkeeper he was more important in Victorian society than he would be today, and there were others like him.

Analysis of the Furness newspapers' correspondence columns suggests that the most important topics were religion, health and highways, with temperance, education and the police well represented. Of most immediate concern to the majority of the population was the question of public health, and health and streets together were the most important topic in Ulverston papers and a good second to religion in Barrow. This is confirmation of the need for the Public Health Act of

1875. There seems little doubt of the importance of local newspapers' role in this field, and it was one in which, more than in any other, they were striving on behalf of the working classes. Indeed, it is hard to see how any historian can emphasise the importance of local initiative in this matter and yet neglect to mention newspapers. Throughout the country there are examples of newspapers focusing attention on the question of sanitation. Reformers had the opportunity to make complaints and were supported in leading articles.

What is striking about the correspondence columns is the great variety of topics and the large numbers of contributors — characteristics paralleled elsewhere. In some cases the historian is taken close to the actual individuals, for example in the following intimate piece of vernacular evidence, a letter written to the *Ulverston Mirror* in 1869 by a miner's wife who wanted changing rooms for the men at the place where her husband worked:

> Many of the men have to walk four miles to their homes drenched in wet, and when they arrive there is only one six-inch firegrate for drying, cooking and doing all the work — not a little in a miner's home. The poor children have to stand behind the smoking garments half-starved and after all our drying the clothes are scarcely fit to put on at such an early hour as half-past two o'clock in the morning.

Simply to write such a letter may well have taken considerable effort. Noise, lack of decent lighting, tiredness and undernourishment were general problems to be overcome. Altick has written of the difficulty, perhaps impossibility, of recreating 'the spirit of so large and inarticulate a community as the English working classes in the nineteenth century', yet an anonymous miner's wife made her voice heard. That she was able to do so at all was due to the existence of a district newspaper.

Another striking feature of the correspondence columns is the often enormous length of the letters. The newspaper-reading public needed the 'power of sustained attention' before World War I.

In the nineteenth century the newspapers' particular distinction was that they were the quickest and only method of communicating news of events and opinions to large numbers of people outside an area covered by the spoken word. Among those Victorians fully appreciative of this fact were Barrow's leading capitalists. To them, 'to make known' were the operative words, especially since their group was making the news, creating new industries and actually controlling the destinies of town and district. They would have agreed with a nineteenth-century editor of the *Spectator* that 'the newspaper is indispensable to progress, and progress in the right direction'. The Furness Railway group gave financial backing for a newspaper to serve Barrow and to publicise it and the efforts of the capitalists. The paper, quantitatively at least, was a not unworthy contemporary of the daily press of Barrow's rivals — Liverpool and Middlesbrough — with which there was 'debate' on matters such as shipping and iron. Printer's ink mapped out the industrial and commercial empire that would take in the country between the Mersey and the Solway. The role of publicist was performed by the *Barrow Herald* as well as by the *Barrow Times*, so that, in championing their town and district, the newspaper which more than any other in the early decades of Barrow's growth sympathised with the working classes also co-operated with the organ of the leading capitalists — a clear example of the local patriotism that could inspire journalists. Both newspapers presented, in the boom years of the early seventies, a boastful picture of Barrow and district. They consistently documented, in 'lyrical language', the growth of the town, emphasising its size, progress and resources, praising the enterprise of capitalists and stressing the good relations between masters and men when, in fact, for its comparatively small size, Barrow was one of the most strike-bound towns in the 1870s. These were characteristics of other Furness newspapers and of those in rival Cleveland, too. In the difficult years of the later seventies, as favourable an image of Barrow as possible was presented: resilience, resources, and stability were emphasised.

Labour relations were the subject of much national interest and of extensive legislation in the mid-Victorian period. Barrow was a proletarian town controlled by a handful of capitalists. In this situation the existence of an independent press was important, as can be briefly illustrated.

In autumn 1871, the weekly pays and nine hours issues came to the fore in Barrow. The *Barrow Herald* had long advocated weekly pays and on 4 November, out of a total of seventeen and a half columns of editorial, just under three columns were devoted to the workmen's agitation, in addition to a long editorial supporting them. During that month, five letters out of nine, totalling nearly 3,000 words, were received from working men on weekly pays and nine hours. One of them thanked the *Herald*, which in the sixties had been used by trade unionists to express their views: 'I assure you, sir, the workmen are exceedingly pleased with the way in which you have placed their views before the public on all occasions. . .' Carruthers in the *Barrow Pilot*, during September, October and November 1871, wrote several long leading articles in support of weekly pays and, like the *Herald*, gave extensive coverage to the course of events. His paper published ten letters on weekly pays during that time, at least eight of which were from working men.

These papers were as much champions of working men at this time as Joseph Cowen's more renowned *Newcastle Daily Chronicle*. In 1875 there was a serious dispute involving the Amalgamated Society of Engineers and the Hindpool Steel Works, during which the *Barrow Times*, primarily anxious about investments and critical of trade unions for their ignorance of political economy and their denial of individual freedom, nevertheless published remarkably full and fair accounts of meetings held by the workmen. Handsome support for the strikers was given by both the *Barrow Pilot* and

the *Vulcan*, which bitterly and lengthily clashed with the
employers' paper, the *Barrow Times*, on the issue, bringing
home to the capitalists the working men's viewpoint, even if
the strikers would seem to have been ultimately unsuccessful.

In spite of the legislation of 1871-6 jubilant unionists failed
to remember that parliamentary acts were interpreted by
courts that were influenced by a common law still hostile to
unions. This unsatisfactory aspect of the situation was reflected in the Furness press. The newspapers emphasised that
they accepted trade unions, and praised their benefit functions. However, there was a good deal about them that they
did not like. Nevertheless, if trade unions (and they represented a minority of the working population) were often criti-
cised, labour had sympathy among the press. When the
employers' newspaper described the effect of the removal of
Barrow's 'curse', as the *Vulcan* desired, it expressed the fact
that in a free-enterprise economy the businessman was the
most important character. S. G. Checkland in *The Rise of
Industrial Society in England, 1815-1885* says: 'It was with
him that the principal initiative lay: his decisions to embark
or to remain passive, and his ability to estimate and manipu-
late, were the proximate determinants of growth and change.'

However, mid-Victorian society did not allow the businessman to reign supreme: he was checked both by the old landed
interest and the new working classes. In Furness, where his
functions were so clearly visible because of the area's dependence upon him, he was also subject to newspaper scrutiny.
Furthermore, the dignity of labour was emphasised. Workmen
are free men, said the radical *Barrow Herald;* the future
depends on labour, not capitalists, prophesied the *Vulcan*; the
workmen 'justly claim to be sentient beings', said the
Ulverston Mirror, and in the newspapers of rival Cleveland
similar points were made. By ensuring that another point of
view was heard and by stressing the dignity of labour newspapers were aiding the process of democratisation.

The provincial press had had a strong Liberal bias for

many years before the newspaper tax was repealed, and this bias was strengthened by the growth of dailies, new weeklies and biweeklies. If the 'new mass press, with the complaisance of its readers, was more an instrument of party than the old . . .', there was no demand for a paper unconnected with an official party. Consequently, a newspaper might claim to be politically independent and yet be a party weapon. Thus the *Lancaster Guardian* quoted Milton as part of its masthead: 'Give me the liberty to know, to utter, and to argue freely, according to conscience', and yet was firmly Liberal. The *Crewe Guardian* could say it was 'Neutral in all Matters Political and Religious', yet its news had a clear Tory bias.

Politically, the emphasis of the Furness press was Liberal, and it is interesting to examine its behaviour in 1880 when the first contested general election occurred locally after the Secret Ballot Act of 1872. The Furness prints, Liberal and Tory, and others in the North Lancashire parliamentary division — traditionally Conservative but now more interesting because of the extension of the franchise and the secret ballot, the growth of Barrow and of other smaller towns and the existence of a vigorous local press — provided very extensive coverage and revealed a total bias both in their expressed attitudes and in their technical handling of events. At the climax of their campaigns, almost saturated with the election topic, they were blatantly propagandist and in their political intolerance they indicated that Britain was as yet far from being a democracy. The bias extended to the meanest paragraph, to the wit and humour columns,[7] and guided each reporter's pen. These were features of newspapers elsewhere, such as in the *Gazette*, the *Guardian* and the *Observer* in Lancaster and the *Gazette* in Blackpool.

The Furness newspapers put a different emphasis upon different issues. This confirms on the one hand that there was not one public opinion but many; on the other, it illustrates that party policy at election time was not clearly defined. There was a marked contrast in the amount of technical advice about voting published by the papers; the Liberals were the political educators, the champions of the newly enfranchised classes.

The bias may be said to have had positive advantages. It brought home the differences between the parties and encouraged, in one area and at grass-roots level, the polarisation of the modern two-party system. The views were so sharply expressed, for example over the candidature of the representatives of two leading territorial families, that the attitudes of deference that Tholfsen has traced must have been undermined throughout the country, if the Furness press was typical. There could be no question of complete confidence in the face of such outspokenness.

Another advantage of bias may be illustrated by the Tory *Vulcan.* This was, in 1880, a feeble publication compared with its rivals. National disparity in numbers, it has been said, was generally reflected in content and circulation of Liberal and Conservative newspapers. However, in the Liberal stronghold of Barrow, even the *Vulcan* made public the views of the other side.

One other aspect of the newspapers is interesting during the election, although it is not confined to such a period. The *Manchester City News* in 1880 actually said that contemporary papers rarely if ever contained any reference to the contents of their fellows, and that each seemed to ignore the existence of the rest. The *City News* may have had in mind the newspapers of London and the larger cities; its comment was wrong in respect of Furness papers. They and others in Lancashire harnessed to their cause extracts from prints of similar persuasion, and in their turn would similarly have been used.

Newspapers were more than news papers, for they carried advertisements as well, which extended their influence beyond their journalistic function. The proprietor as advertiser was perhaps as important as the proprietor as journalist, and the newspaper as shop window as important as the newspaper

as critic. Normally, when the historian thinks of advertising
and newspapers, he thinks of the dangerous dependence of
newspapers upon advertisements and the counter-argument
that only through the growth of advertising would the press
achieve independence. Liberty of the press is fundamental,
but not exclusive; advertisements themselves are as important
as the revenue they bring because advertisers are not talking
to posterity but to the men and women of their own time;
yet many history texts seem to disregard their importance.
Advertising was to expand rapidly in the last decades of the
nineteenth century; and whatever the arguments for and
against, it has become an important aspect of everyday life.
Grass-roots newspapers, among others, contributed to the
increasing acceptance of advertising which, in part at least,
caused that expansion.

Basic to any assessment of the benefits of newspaper
advertising is an understanding of its nature. In *Advertising
and the Public*, Harris and Seldon wrote: 'All advertisements
are calls to action of one kind or another. They make no sense
unless addressed to people with freedom to decide for themselves the pattern of their work and lives.' The increased newspaper advertising of the mid-Victorian period came at a time
when increasing numbers of the population were improving
their lot, although many members of the working classes still
lacked much that would enable them to live in comfort and
dignity. During this period, when shops were switching from
fulfilling needs to creating wants, an examination of advertisement columns in the newspapers of, say, Barrow or St Helens
can reveal the bitter competition of retailers.

> They contain notices from those who have just arrived and
> announcements from those who have moved on to large
> and better-situated premises — and from the assignees of
> those who have failed. Everyone was on the move,
> either up or out.[8]

Other features of the advertisement columns were the solicitous phraseology of the advertisers 'humbly asking for the patronage of all classes', phraseology which may have contributed to an increasing dignity among the working classes.

The enterprising could also use newspapers to seek employment. True, this was not a new service, but it became more important when advertisements were cheaper and local newspapers proliferated, and when the labour market was haphazardly organised. The lower middle classes and some at least of the working classes wanted opportunities to better themselves and thus to rise in the social scale. The more opportunities there were the better. In Furness, individuals from places as far away as Liverpool and Manchester used the opportunity to advertise for employment, mostly for clerical jobs and posts in domestic service, thus reflecting significant national economic trends. Getting on was stressed in Victorian England, and what it meant in individual terms can be glimpsed in the situations wanted columns: an eighteen-year-old girl with three years' experience as a dressmaker wanting to be 'an assistant in the higher branches of domestic duties' in a genteel family; a young man claiming to have a 'perfect knowledge' of drapery after having been in the business for five years. Another's advertisement aptly bridged two economic structures: 'A good scholar and could manage a horse.' Despite the fact that mid-Victorians were experiencing the first application of power-driven machinery to transport on an extensive scale, the horse still appeared in the situations wanted and vacant columns.

Interestingly, just as major employers and others used the advertisement columns to find labour, 'steady' labour, so workmen used those columns to warn other workmen to stay away to prevent any strike breaking. The *Barrow Times*, whose economics were orthodox and whose owners were major capitalists, allowed this advertisement to appear: 'To Joiners — Wanted, Joiners to keep away from Ulverston during the strike.' The vocabulary of the situations wanted and vacant columns is illuminating, too. Although by the

1870s, if not earlier, the derogatory term 'hands' does not seem to have been used in leading articles in the Furness press, it was still used in advertisements.

Analysis of the sources of products and services advertised show that, in spite of the importance of London, whose influence was steadily increasing, a growing number of provincial centres appeared in the advertisements. Within these columns can be traced, therefore, over the span of years, an extending environment: in this way newspapers contributed to the breaking down of the barriers of ignorance and tradition. Even the reader of a small local newspaper could put himself at the terminal point of an increasingly intricate network of communications about products, the variety of which would increase towards the end of the century and thus lessen the dominance of patent medicines and pure tea!

In spite of, to the modern eye, a drab appearance, minuteness of print, tendency to verbose expression and varying amounts of second-hand information, the local papers were a vigorous and interesting part of local society. Their precise influence will remain unknown. It is wrong to accept without question what papers said about themselves, and readers of contemporary records therefore often despair of reference to the press. However, to take but one example of its kind, the *Liverpool Mercury* and *Daily Courier* were well aware of their Barrow contemporary which was making such an effort to become known, even to the extent where scissors and paste were used upon Ramsden's *Times* and the lyrical language of Furness appeared in the commercial pages. As for elections such as that of 1880, one must not be obsessed with actual election results. Leach, of the *Barrow Times*, was anxious lest secret voting, in removing the excitement of open voting, should cause people to neglect their duty, but here was precisely the newspaper's function: to put issues before the voters; distinguish between the parties; rally the committed and reinforce their views; and, perhaps most important of all, to put people in a voting frame of mind. Even now the reader can recapture the excitement of the time in their pages. Moreover, correspondents' letters elicited replies; rival newspapers, whether they belonged to the same or different towns, argued with one another, and although circulations were often small the range of circulation needs also to be borne in mind when assessing their influence, as some were available over very wide areas.

Whether the newspapers created or reinforced or reflected opinion mattered little. What was important was that thoughts and attitudes (and also facts, such as information about ironworks and shipyards) were made public; that there were frames of reference which inhabitants could accept, or modify, or reject; that there were lines of communication open to all to use, whatever their opinions, whatever their social status. A district with newspapers was healthier than a district without.

In a Commons debate in 1860, Lord Robert Cecil decried the newspapers as educators because he had a rigid idea as to what education meant. Another speaker's words in that same debate suggested another process of learning and communication:

> Education does not entirely consist in what is learned at the mother's knee, or in the book at school; it is going on every day of one's life, and principally through the medium of newspapers, even of the cheap newspapers. . .[9]

Notes to this chapter are on pages 188-9

Chapter Five

The Victorian Entrepreneur in Lancashire

J. H. Fox

The growth of the Lancashire textile industry is often
explained in terms of favourable geographical, climatic and
economic conditions, but while these are obviously vital, the
importance of the entrepreneurs should not be overlooked.
It was these men who succeeded in making use of the opportunities offered by favourable conditions, and their social
origins and careers are the subject of this chapter.

In attempting to analyse the social origins and careers of
Lancashire entrepreneurs, a group of seventy has been chosen.
Certain criteria were applied in their selection, one being that
all were born between 1805 and 1835, and were thereby in
business during all or part of Queen Victoria's reign. Only
textile entrepreneurs have been included, although this field
has been taken to include not only the manufacture of
materials such as cotton, silk and fustians, but also such
related industries as textile machine making, the preliminary
and finishing processes of textile production, hat manufacture
and so on. Those who inherited a textile business from their
fathers have not been included, as the concern here is with
those who either set up new businesses or became proprietors

of existing ones with which they had no parental connection. However, entrepreneurs who began separate businesses themselves have been included, together with those who inherited a business from a relative other than a father. In most cases these careers have been traced through obituaries in trade magazines and local newspapers, and only if the occupation of an entrepreneur's father has been stated in one of these sources has that person been eligible for inclusion. Thus, while this group is not a random sample in the statistical sense, neither has it been chosen on the basis of the social class into which that person was born, nor according to the way in which he eventually became a proprietor.

Social origins played an important part in determining which men were most likely to succeed in business and, indeed, which were most likely to attempt a business career. These origins would be determined by the occupation of the male head of the family. (A list of the occupations of the fathers of these entrepreneurs is found in the appendix.) In this way the proportions of entrepreneurs from the middle and lower classes has been determined. According to Patrick Colquhoun's division of society in 1803, those from the middle classes included the owners of businesses, managers (including foremen), farmers and professional men, while factory operatives, labourers and such like belonged to the working classes. Of seven handloom weavers, one, Joseph Pickles, was the owner of a business based on this trade. He set up as draper so that he could sell his wares and consequently is considered here as having been the owner of a business. Many handloom weavers were comparable to factory operatives in that the raw material was given to them by a merchant, who also paid them for the cloth that they produced. In this way six of the seven handloom weavers have been classified as being of working class origin, though in some cases it is not clear if they were employed by merchants; this is therefore a possible source of error. By the above method of classification fifty-four families were from the middle classes and sixteen from the working classes.

This can be compared with the structure of the society into which these entrepreneurs were born. Colquhoun's estimate of the relative sizes of the social orders in 1803 suggests that 67 per cent of the families in England and Wales belonged to the lower classes and 31.6 per cent to the middle classes.[1] The Census of 1841, though detailed, does not set out the occupations of the people in quite the most useful way for the purpose required here, as it does not always distinguish between masters and workmen. Professor Harrison concludes from this census that the labouring classes in Great Britain (some of the entrepreneurs being born in Scotland) formed 'a very high percentage of the total population'; and probably a figure of 75 per cent would not be too inaccurate. It can be seen quite clearly that a man born into the middle classes was far more likely to become the owner of a business than one who had begun his life in a family lower down the social scale.

One reason for this is that, the higher up the social scale, the better the start in life that parents could ensure for their sons, and the more help they were able to give them later. One of the best ways in which assistance could be given to an aspiring factory owner was by giving or loaning him capital. A good education, good business connections and social status were amongst other advantages with which the sons of middle-class families were endowed. Working-class families were far less able to help their children in similar or other ways.

Businessmen were well able to supply their sons with capital. The career of G. B. Neild owed much to his father, John Neild of the Crown and Anchor Inn in Oldham.[2] G. B. Neild began his business in cotton spinning after he had worked as a bookkeeper and later in a warehouse. The money with which he and his brother Phineas extended the business was given to them by their father. Thomas Broadbent Wood, after he had received a good education, was sent as an

105

apprentice to the firm of Radcliffe Bros of Rochdale. On completing his apprenticeship he worked for John Harrington and Co, warehousemen, where he gained a good grounding in running a business. Wood's father, a banker, then bought for him Park Mill in Middleton, which Thomas ran as a highly successful cotton-spinning concern. Professional men also were able to help their sons financially; indeed, some provided such aid on a very generous scale. William Whittam finally succeeded in persuading his father to send him to a cotton manufacturer in Bolton to learn the cotton business. When William had received the requisite amount of knowledge on the subject his father, Joseph, built Mossfield Mill in New Bury and himself gave up his legal career to go into cotton manufacturing with William and the latter's two younger brothers. When Joseph died in 1876, William inherited his part of the works.

Some men were fortunate enough to inherit a business from their fathers, using capital from this in order to embark on a textile career. This is what happened to the Taylor brothers of Wigan.[3] James Taylor, the father, owned a tannery business at Billinge, and when he died in 1836 his sons carried on the concern. The two sons who played the greatest part in running the business were James and Thomas, who together built the first cotton-spinning mills in Wallgate. A third brother, Richard, joined the firm later, though by training he was a surgeon. A similar type of career was followed by James Folds of Burnley, whose father was a builder and contractor. He was educated at Burnley Grammar School and then entered his father's business, which with his brother he inherited in 1834. Ten years later the brothers went into the cotton trade at Rishton Mill.

A father in an influential position would have been able to give great assistance to the advancement of his son's career. The manager of a factory was in a position to ensure that his son was given a job in the establishment of which he had charge, and no doubt promotion prospects for that son were better than they were for most of the other employees. Samuel Barlow's father was the manager of the bleachworks of Otho Hulme and Sons, Medlock Vale, at which works Samuel first commenced work.[4] When his father became manager of the bleaching department of the Adelphi Print Works, Salford, Barlow junior was sent into the colour-mixing department as an apprentice. In 1847 the father became manager of the bleachworks at Stakehill then occupied by Heald, Wilson and Co, and so Samuel, who at the time was unemployed, went to work there also. He succeeded to the position of manager when his father died in 1855. Eventually the owners gave up the business and Samuel, together with others, became the new proprietors of the works, then renamed Samuel Barlow and Co.

Well educated men of good social background did not begin their careers when six or seven years old on the factory floor. These men would start work later in life and further up the promotional ladder. Richard Hermon was a small country gentleman whose son, Edward, the Member of Parliament for Preston from 1868 until his death in 1881, was such an example. Edward received a good education before being engaged in the London warehouse of Horrockses, Miller and Co, the famous Preston firm. By the age of twenty-four he was principal clerk, and in 1861 he became a partner in the company.

Another advantage of good social status was that it increased the chances of marrying into a business family or of being born into a family that had relatives in the business world. William Whittam married the daughter of Thomas Lewis Livsey, the proprietor of a print works, and inherited part of this on his father-in-law's death, which occurred some time after Whittam had started his own business. John Harley's career is described later, but, from a middle-class family, he married the owner's daughter and inherited her father's works. Robert Hopwood Hutchinson's father, a land surveyor, married the daughter of the founder of the

extensive Nova Scotia Mills in Blackburn, and not only
inherited a fortune from his mother, but also eventually became
the principal of those mills.

At the lower end of the middle classes, families were not
able to assist their sons' careers very much, if at all. Henry
Ward's father was a barber in Blackburn, but his business
yielded such a small income that he found it difficult to feed
and clothe his family.[5] Henry did not receive much of an
education, though he was taught the family trade, which he
took up as a career while at the same time carrying on a bit
of independent trading which enabled him to save £80 by
the time he was eighteen. Eventually he became a cotton
manufacturer and by the time the American Civil War broke
out he was quite a wealthy man. It was during this war that
he was reputed to have made nearly £1 million by running
the cotton blockade of the South. When he was fifteen,
James Jardine left the family farm near Bury to seek employment elsewhere. The only qualifications he had at
that time was an 'education' from the nearby village school.
After working on his father's farm at Great Harwood, William
Birtwistle left to become an apprentice shoemaker at
Whalley.

At the bottom end of the social scale it was often not a
question of what help a father could give to his son, but
rather what contribution a son could make to the upkeep of
the family. John Walmsley was a handloom weaver and the
father of fifteen children.[6] One of his sons, also named John,
had no schooling and began work when only seven years of
age as a bobbin-winder for handloom weavers. Similarly, Eli
Higham, before he was seven years old, was sent to the mill
to learn how to weave. While he was still a half-timer his
father, a factory worker, was killed, leaving Eli as the bread-
winner. An equally hard beginning in life was experienced by
John Fish who became a bobbin-winder for his parents, who
were handloom weavers, when he was only five years old.
Three years later John himself had progressed to the handloom

on which he continued until his father died, after which both John, then sixteen, and his mother went to work in a mill.

Occasionally, though, such families were able to furnish assistance. John Jackson and a younger brother, Luther, were enabled to start in business only because the family savings were placed at their disposal. Their father was a handloom weaver with eight children to support. Poor home circumstances explain why many sons from the working classes failed to become business owners, but they also make more remarkable the achievement of those who succeeded.

It has already been suggested that a reasonable education was more likely to be the prerogative of entrepreneurs from the middle classes. Only one of the entrepreneurs, William Muir, was connected with a university. While employed in Glasgow he attended classes at the university and also took an active part in the formation of the Glasgow Mechanics' Institute, of which he was one of the first subscribing members. A grammar-school education was received by, amongst others, James Folds, Robert T. Heape, Henry Whalley and John Goodair. This was not of direct use to the aspiring entrepreneur, as the grammar-school curriculum was usually dominated by the classics at that time. The Sunday school at Castleshaw Spout provided Morgan Brierley with 'the better part of his education', while John Haworth of Accrington '. . . was sent to a school in Duncan Square kept by old Mrs Tattersall. There were about twenty scholars, who were taught in the back kitchen, which was not flagged'. Half-timers like Eli Higham would possibly have known something of the 3 Rs; others, like William Hoyle and James Beads, had to resort to night school and private study after work if they wished to become reasonably literate. An illiterate man would have been considerably handicapped in running a business or in raising himself above the depressed condition of the masses.

The father's aid, though important, must not be allowed to overshadow the achievement of the son. Even men who were given capital had to begin or develop a business and had to run it successfully. There were, of course, many men who had to depend entirely on their own efforts if they wished to become owners of prospering concerns. Such men may have come from very poor families that were unable to assist their children's careers, or they may have decided that the family's help was unnecessary.

It may be appropriate at this point to turn from the parents to the entrepreneurs themselves and, in particular, to the varied careers that they followed. These careers have been divided into six groups, depending on a man's occupation immediately prior to his starting a business in textiles, in order to define the differences between them more clearly, but it must be remembered that few careers were exactly alike, so that any classification can only be approximate.

The first type of career is that in which a man became a partner in or owner of an established business in which he had worked in a lesser capacity for some time. The great advantage of this was that it was not necessary to have enough capital with which to start a business, nor was it necessary to go through the difficult process of building up a business from nothing. It was quite possible for a man to inherit a business on the death of the owner or, on account of his considerable managerial skill, to be taken into partnership, though at least some of those to whom this occurred could have set up in business on their own. At fifteen Archibald Winterbottom entered the firm of Henry Bannerman and Sons of Manchester, and through rapid promotion became a manager when only nineteen and a partner at thirty.[7] After having been taken into partnership Winterbottom opened a warehouse on his own account in 1853, but in 1869 the business failed. Later he became a very successful manufacturer at Weaste and in 1882 was able to repay the £20,000 that he owed from the failure in 1869.

Philip Gillibrand was employed at Henry Bannerman's as a clerk in the counting house but, like Winterbottom, eventually rose to the position of partner in the firm, which he left to take up a directorship in Salford.

If the owner happened to be a relative, then promotion to the position of partner would probably have been somewhat more assured. So Joseph Lamb had been sent by his parents to learn about spindle and fly-making, but when his brother John began his own business Joseph joined him and was eventually taken into partnership. When John died three years after Joseph had become a partner the latter inherited the business as the nearest living relative of his unmarried brother. In a similar way, Robert Taylor Heape inherited a business of wool merchants with which he had been connected for some time and which had warehouses in Rochdale. Originally the firm was known as Messrs Butterworth and Heape, but on the retirement of Butterworth and the death of Robert Heape, the son of Robert Taylor Heape's great-grandfather, the business passed into Robert Taylor Heape's hands. He then renamed the firm Messrs R. T. Heape and Son.

The entrepreneurs in the second group worked in an establishment connected with one of the textile trades and then left to set up a business of their own. Some started work in the factory at a very young age performing menial tasks, while others began later in life in rather better jobs. Similarly, some left the factory to start on their own when still only operatives, while some had been managers for a few years before they decided that the time had come to set up in business. There were those whose parents gave them money and those who had to rely on their own hard earned savings.

Only a relatively small number of men followed the type of career that received so much publicity in Victorian England: the career from rags to riches which began in poverty on the shop floor and ended in wealth as the owner of a prosperous business. Such careers were, indeed, remarkable, for the effort required to overcome all the obstacles called for men of great character and ability.

One of the fortunate few who did progress from rags to

riches was William Hoyle,[8] who was born in 1831 of humble parents (his father was a factory operative), and began work as a half-timer in Hamer's Mill, Brooksbottom at the age of eight. Five years later he was old enough to work full time, which meant that he had to continue his education at night school and through private study. It was usual for him to get up at three o'clock in the morning in order to pursue his studies, which were resumed at night after he returned from work. In 1853 William and his father joined his father's cousin in business at Crawshawbooth with what little money they had managed to save between them. The venture was not a success in the first few years — by 1857 they were £46 worse off than they had been at the outset, because of the adverse economic situation. After that, however, as the economic climate improved the business began to make money. Subsequently they left Crawshawbooth and erected a mill in Tottington which was twice extended.

One of Hoyle's characteristics, which no doubt contributed to his success, was his abstemiousness, a characteristic nurtured by his Wesleyan Methodist upbringing. He was fifteen when he signed the pledge, and he played an important part in the temperance movement locally. At Tottington he paid his workers an extra shilling a week in lieu of drink. Later he became a vegetarian. Even when he was running a thousand looms, the household expenses for himself, his wife and two children did not exceed £100 a year. Unless a man born in very poor circumstances was able to make great sacrifices, he would be unlikely to find enough capital with which to start a business and then to expand it.

James Beads, a spinner's son, was sent to work when eleven years old as a creeler in the spinning room, where he remained for eight years. Like Hoyle, Beads was most eager to obtain some kind of an education so, after his twelve-hour day, which ended at 8 pm, he went to night school. His second job was as timekeeper in a factory, and after that he became a bookkeeper in the warehouse at the Commercial Mills, Nova

Scotia. He then set up in business as a cotton manufacturer and after an initial failure re-entered the cotton trade in 1871 to become a successful mill owner. This emphasises the importance of economic conditions. Beads failed the first time because there had been insufficient time for him to make his business strong enough to survive a stagnant period in the economy, in this case brought about by the cotton famine. Again, he was a member of the Methodist Church.

A final example of one who began life in a very humble capacity is provided by John Haworth, who began his working life when only six as a tear boy, normally working fourteen hours a day for 1s 6d a week. From there he progressed to the dye house, then to the grey-room, and eventually to the colour shop where, owing to his great interest in chemistry (which had been fostered by the classes in that subject at the works), he became foreman. On leaving this firm, which was owned by James Simpson, Haworth became colour-mixer for Nathan Lloyd, after which he went to Bradshaw Hall as foreman of the colour shop. It was after this that he commenced in business with a partner to make the then new coal-tar colours of mauve and magenta. One of the reasons for Haworth's success was his knowledge of chemistry, which he applied to the making of dyes, and his strength of character in pursuing his study of it.

The three men described above are all extreme examples, in that they began right at the bottom of the ladder. Most of those in this group, however, began in the factory somewhat higher up. Joseph Schofield's first job was as office boy in the counting house of a mill in Oldham, and he began in business on his own after he had risen to the position of cashier. Unlike the sons of poorer families he was able to remain at school until he was about fourteen. It was at Wood Mill, Newhey, that Benjamin Brierley carried on his business carding wool for those who were unable to do so on their own premises. Brierley's sons used to help their father in the business, but Morgan decided to become a fancy flannel manufacturer, which he did first in Wardleworth and later in Rochdale. Those who began their working lives in a factory or mill in a reasonable job had a fair chance of rising to a position from which they could attempt to branch out on their own; men who began in the lowest jobs rarely rose to such a position.

A slight, though important, variation of the above career was that of the man who became manager of a mill and, after having held this position for a while, set up his own business. It was quite possible that the manager was in sole charge of the mill, in the running of which the owner might have played a very small part. Accordingly, the manager, instead of being paid a fixed salary, might have been paid according to the quantity of work turned out in the mill.[9] In this way a manager would have had a good chance of procuring sufficient capital to start in business on quite a large scale. Samuel Brooks, for example, was the sole manager of the commercial department in the firm of Messrs Elce and Cottam, cotton machinists. On the death of John Elce, Brooks became the general manager of the works under the supervision of the trustees. He had only held this post for a short time when he decided to start his own business. In one room of a mill he installed machines with which to manufacture loom temples and accessories and also to repair cotton machinery. At first he employed about six men. Though this was small in comparison with what the business developed into later, it was quite large for an initial enterprise.

Another advantage of being a manager is shown by the career of Matthew Curtis, the manager of the wire-card branch of the famous firm of machinists owned by J. C. Dyer. For some reason Dyer decided to sell the wire-card section of his business and gave Curtis, as manager, the option of buying it. Curtis accepted the offer and bought it together with a Mr Parr, one of Dyer's travellers. In the same way Curtis and Parr acquired the machine-making part of Dyer's business and here they were joined by Mr Madeley, who had been manager of that department. It need hardly be stated that the experience gained in running a mill through being its manager would have been of great value when coming to own a business of one's own.

Many entrepreneurs were faced with the task of beginning a business in the cheapest possible way, as they had not enough capital to buy or build factories or to instal in them a considerable amount of machinery. One way of cutting down on costs was to rent accommodation for the machinery and also to buy power to drive the machines from the owner of the building. This deferred the purchasing of premises, the cost of which could later be met from the profits of the business. John Jackson began his business in Rochdale with twenty-two looms. He paid a shilling per week per loom, a price which included the use of a building and steam power. After twelve years in these premises Jackson, who was in partnership with his brother, built the Trafalgar Street Mill. Premises in Ashworth Street, Blackburn were occupied by John Fish as a sub-tenant.

If a firm went bankrupt then its property was sold at less than the market value, so that a mill or machinery could be purchased relatively cheaply. According to George Smith of Manchester this was a good way of embarking in the business of spinning and manufacturing.[10] A mill in Moses Gate was bought by John Hindley on the failure of a Mr Openshaw, to whom the mill formerly belonged. At the time Hindley was already in business with two partners. Eli Higham, a cotton waste dealer of Accrington, was owed a large amount of money by a cotton manufacturer who was unable to pay the debt. The manufacturer suggested that Higham should take over the mill in lieu of cash. Higham agreed to this and took James Jackson as his partner in the venture. John Mitchell and his partners even bought an old gasworks in which they installed 150 looms for the manufacture of cotton velvet. The vast majority of entrepreneurs began their business careers in partnerships, another way of reducing the amount of money that one man had to find: the savings of William Hoyle, his father and the latter's cousin were combined when they became partners.

Relatives were sometimes of importance in the formation of partnerships. Richard Bell was a cashier at Peel Lane Mills, Heywood, until his brother-in-law became the tenant of a mill in Tottington, upon which the brothers-in-law became partners in business. After having worked in a mill for a number of years Daniel Arkwright in 1839 entered into a partnership with his brother-in-law, John Parkinson Parke of Withnell. In 1852 Arkwright started a mill in Preston on his own account.

Sometimes a man would be taken into partnership on account of his ability in running a business. After having worked for thirty years, part of which time as head of a department, in Salis Schwabe's firm, Henry Whalley left to join in partnership with Allen Mellor and Co at Grimshaw Mill, Middleton Junction. There Whalley was the chief manager, and later he became a director of the Middleton and Tonge Cotton Mill Company. Similarly, Thomas Lancashire was in charge of a silk warehouse in Leigh before he became the 'resident partner' in the firm of Messrs Harrop, Taylor and Pearson which owned Brook Mill in Leigh. For these two men business acumen served as a substitute for capital.

Not everybody was engaged in textiles from the very beginning of his business career. Some began in a different business and only later developed an interest in textiles, either continuing in their original business as well, or becoming solely concerned with textiles. These men have been placed in group three. Some, if not all, the capital with which these men began textile businesses derived from their previous businesses. The fortunate minority simply inherited a business from their fathers; most began life in rather less advantageous circumstances.

Shopkeeping seems to have been the most common business carried on by these entrepreneurs immediately before their branching out into textiles. Grocers were particularly prevalent, though this type of shop was the commonest sort within the community. In 1843 Joseph Woods entered into business on his own account as a grocer and tobacconist in Preston. He was so successful in this that in 1867 he became a partner in a cotton-manufacturing business, though he also continued with his shop. John Walmsley had been a handloom weaver before he began in business as a grocer and continued this for fifteen years. Then in 1850, he built a weaving shed which at first contained eighty-four looms. From that time the business developed until he owned a spinning mill with 29,000 spindles and a weaving shed with 354 looms. When the spinning mill was destroyed by fire in 1886 the damage was estimated at £20,000, which suggests just how profitable his business was. John Halliwell inherited a grocer's shop from his father after which he began cotton manufacturing in partnership with three others, by leasing an old mill in Darwen and installing sixty-six looms in it. In Colne Henry Pickles and his brothers inherited a handloom weaving and drapery business from their father. This business was greatly expanded through the efforts of the family, especially Henry, until finally they began to employ power looms for making the cloth. Henry invested the wealth that he acquired in various textile companies.

Other businesses that textile entrepreneurs were initially engaged upon included insurance, building, auctioneering, coal shipping and tanning. Richard Haworth's career was in many respects similar to those of Hoyle, Beads and John Haworth. His father, a working man, was killed in an accident, so that the burden of providing for and bringing up the eight children fell on Haworth's mother, to whose training he attributed much of his later success in business.[11] The young Haworth was sent to work when twelve years old but injured his hand in an accident while cleaning his loom, so that he was unable to carry on weaving. After the accident he was employed in keeping the accounts of the winders and dressers

before he took up an appointment as a bookkeeper for
Rylands and Sons. Later he became a bookkeeper, then
cashier, for another firm, and he also kept the books of a
building club in the evenings for 1s 6d a week in order to
earn extra money. His first business was in insurance in
Manchester under the name of Hulton and Haworth. A third
partner joined the firm when they began as yarn agents and
they also opened a trade in dyed goods for the London
market. Egerton Mills were built from the profits the firm
realised by using the opportunities presented by the
American Civil War to its advantage. Like Hoyle, Haworth did
not spend very much on personal expenses, being a man who
believed in 'a small house and a big factory'. He was reputed
to have said that 'the eyes of other people are the eyes that
ruin us. If all but myself were blind, I should want neither
fine clothes, fine houses, nor fine furniture.' As a Wesleyan
Methodist he had a strong puritan streak in him (many
amusements which he deemed frivolous were not allowed in
his household), from which he could have derived the
strength of character that enabled him to succeed in business
despite a poor start in life.

One of the least common ways of becoming the owner of
a successful business was to marry the owner's daughter. Only
one man (who constitutes group four) from the sample
became an entrepreneur solely because he married the daughter
of a factory owner. This one man was John Harley,[12] whose
career prior to inheriting the business included being an
itinerant preacher in the Wesleyan Church and a shop
assistant. While preaching in Rochdale he married the
daughter of William Standring, a spring and doffing-plate
manufacturer. Standring retired from business and each of
his sons in turn ran it for a time before he died. This left only
John Harley to take over the firm, which he did, eventually
becoming its owner when Standring died. (After starting his
business career Harley preached only occasionally!) His was
an unusual career in that he had no conscious desire to

become an entrepreneur — the role was thrust upon him by chance.

Those entrepreneurs (group five) with the type of mind that could invent new or better machines were well fitted for a career in textiles. The most usual trade that these men entered was textile machine making, though this was not always the case. A man with an invention could either try to find somebody who would provide the money to put it into production, or try to do this on his own. It all depended on how rich the inventor happened to be. In its day 'the patent coiler' — movable cans for coiling cotton — was used almost universally in the industry, and the inventors, Tatham and Cheetham, derived great profits from it. John Tatham served an apprenticeship as a mechanic at Bright's in Rochdale and then joined with Cheetham in business. The profits from the coiler enabled the pair to expand considerably in the field of textile machine making. The training of William Muir in machine and tool making consisted of an apprenticeship and several years as a foreman at both Maudslay and Field's and Bramah and Robinson's, two famous London firms. In 1842 he began to work for a stationmaster called Edmondson, who wanted to produce machinery that would improve the handling of railway tickets. Edmondson had at first asked Joseph Whitworth to help him, but Whitworth was not interested and suggested Muir, who at the time was working at Whitworth's. A building was rented jointly by the two men, Edmondson printing the tickets and Muir making the machines for printing, dating and other processes. As this business became more profitable Muir turned his attention increasingly to general machine making, until eventually he left Edmondson and built the Britannia Works in Manchester. One of his inventions in textiles was an automatic machine for winding cotton balls and bobbins which was used extensively in the trade. In this field of business, success invariably went to those who not only made good machinery but also introduced time- and labour-saving innovations.

A final example from this group also serves to show how a business could be developed gradually. Thomas Watson, the sixth of seventeen children, was born at Galgate where his father, William, was the manager of some silk mills.[13] As William's family grew up they were put to work in various departments of his mills, and there Thomas rose to the position of sub-manager. While at the silk mills he invented a device which superseded the boiling of the silk by using steam for the process instead. Despite the saving to the firm of at least £130 a year the owners refused to raise Thomas's pay, so he left and went to Rochdale in 1846 where he worked in a hat-making firm. When this concern went bankrupt Watson and two other employees of the firm (George Healey and James Taylor), with a combined capital of under £500, began to make plush silk and hats in a warehouse. At first they bought the silk yarn and had it woven on handlooms. As the firm progressed a second warehouse was taken in which a few power looms were run, and later still, in 1851, they took a mill in Union Street and spun their own yarn. The initial success of the business was due to one of Watson's inventions, which enabled the hat plush to be finished by machines — an operation formerly done by hand. By being able to produce the plush more cheaply Watson and his partners could under-cut the prices of competitors. As the firm expanded the manufacture of silk velvets was added and success in making a silk velvet from spun silk gave further impetus to the expansion of the business. Taylor died in 1851, and in 1863 Healey retired, having made a fortune, after which the firm became known as Thomas Watson and Company.

The sixth and final group includes only two men, neither of whom owned a business themselves immediately before becoming owners of a textile business, or were employed by a firm that was connected in any way with textiles. One, Thomas Livsey, was apprenticed to a miller before he joined two other men in setting up a cotton spinning mill. The other, Robert Shaw, worked for a time on the farm of which his father was steward and moved from there to become a clerk in a corn mill his uncle owned.[14] It was at this time that he began a business with his brother-in-law Hoyle by running 300 looms in Victoria Mill, Colne Lane. We are told that Robert Shaw had 'not much capital except the savings of his own industry'. When Hoyle retired another brother-in-law, Philips, became Shaw's partner. After about seven years, however, Shaw decided that he preferred to run a business on his own and, accordingly, the partnership was dissolved and Shaw moved his share of the machinery into another mill. The business expanded rapidly and finally reached a total of 2,638 looms and 82,000 spindles (compared with 300 looms at the outset of his business career). It was said that Shaw owed much to running the blockade during the American Civil War, though this is denied by his obituarist.

The table following lists the number of entrepreneurs in each of the groups discussed above and thus their occupation immediately prior to becoming textile entrepreneurs.

Group 1		9
2		29
3		22
4		1
5		5
6		2
Unclear		2
	Total	70

The most striking feature of the table is that the vast majority of textile entrepreneurs had had some previous connections with that industry. The nine men in group 1 worked their ways up to become partners or sole proprietors. All in group 2 worked in a textile establishment (most because they had to, a few because of the training this gave) before they attempted to start a textile business. In group 3 seven men had jobs in textiles before they began in business in another field and later returned to textiles as proprietors. Of the inventors (group 5) four out of the five worked in mills or workshops before their inventions made them successful businessmen. All these textile entrepreneurs were to a greater or lesser extent produced by that industry. The remaining men had no connections with the textile industry until they became proprietors. Those not yet referred to in group 3 consist of eight who worked in jobs unconnected with textiles before setting up a business, again not in textiles, as an intermediate stage to becoming a textile entrepreneur. Marrying the owner's daughter (group 4) does not appear to have been a very successful way of inheriting a business, possibly because, as with John Harley's father-in-law, the business passed first to the sons of the proprietor (if he had any) and only if they died did the sons-in-law come into the reckoning. One inventor, Mark Knowles of Blackburn, was an accountant before he began textile machine making. It was very rare for men who worked in other than textile establishments (group 6) to begin a textile business without first having been in business in some other line. These men would have had little, if any, knowledge of textiles and no more experience in running a business. Men with this background were more likely to have started a business in a field with which they were familiar, as did the eight in group 3 already mentioned. Both in group 6 were in partnership at the outset of their business careers and this could have overcome their lack of necessary knowledge and expertise. The most common training for textile entrepreneurs appears to have included experience in either textiles or business or both.

From the description and analysis of the careers of these seventy entrepreneurs, it can be concluded that there was no one way of reaching the top, though there are some similarities in the routes taken. Before owning a textile business nearly all had had experience in that trade or had owned a business in another field. Also, the majority of their fathers were either in business (some in textiles) or had worked in the textile trade in some capacity, with the latter category being much smaller than the former. The trading and manufacturing sections of the middle ranks of society were producing a much larger number of textile entrepreneurs than any other. Though examples can be given of textile entrepreneurs who did not fit into either of the above patterns, they constituted a minority.

There were other factors that went into the making of a successful entrepreneur — religion, education, family, inventive ability and even sheer luck. Success cannot be attributed to any one factor, but to a combination of factors which differed in both degree and kind from case to case. Thus, religion may have played the dominant role in William Hoyle's rise from factory operative to manufacturer, but in the careers of Thomas Watson and John Harley — like Hoyle both Wesleyans — it played a comparatively minor role. In the last resorts the men who made Lancashire would have attributed their success to their own efforts, for they prided themselves on being self-made men.

Notes to this chapter are on page 189

Appendix
Entrepreneurs whose parents were from the middle classes

Name	Father's occupation	Location*
Arkwright, Daniel	Wholesale grocer	Preston
Barlow, James	Farmer and manufacturer	Bolton
Barlow Samuel	Works manager	Middleton
Barlow, Thomas	Farmer	Bury
Bell, Richard	Farmer	Heywood
Birtwistle, William	Farmer	Blackburn
Booth, Thomas	Chemist and druggist	Rochdale
Brierley, Morgan	Country carder	Rochdale
Brooks, Samuel	Farmer	Manchester
Cooper, George	Grocer and draper	Manchester
Curtis, Matthew	Currier and leather dealer	Manchester
Folds, James	Builder and contractor	Burnley
Gillibrand, Philip	Partner in cotton firm	Manchester
Goodair, John	Merchant	Preston
Grafton, William	Merchant	Manchester
Halliwell, James	Grocer	Darwen
Harley, John	Captain, merchant navy	Rochdale
Heape, Robert T.	Wholesale grocer	Rochdale
Hermon, Edward	Country gentleman	Preston
Hindley, John	Farmer	Bolton
Hutchinson, Robert H.	Land surveyor	Blackburn
Humber, William	Corn merchant	Preston

* The place given is that in whose newspapers the obituary of the entrepreneur may be found. It is not necessarily where the entrepreneur had his business.

Name	Father's occupation	Location
Hurst, Richard	Cotton spinning business	Rochdale
Isherwood, Joseph	Grocer	Preston
Jardine, James	Farmer	Manchester
Jones, James	Works manager	Middleton
Lamb, Joseph	Mechanical business	Manchester
Lancashire, Thomas	Receiver and agent to dean and chapter of Manchester	Bolton
Lewis, James	Grocer	Blackburn
Livsey, Thomas	Blacksmith	Rochdale
Mellor, Allen	Innkeeper and grocer	Middleton
Muir, William	Businessman	Manchester
Neild, G. B.	Innkeeper	Oldham
Parker, James	Farmer	Preston
Pickles, Henry	Handloom weaver and draper	Colne and Nelson
Pilkington, William	Cotton and yarn merchant	Blackburn
Rawcliffe, John	Owned various businesses	Preston
Schofield, Joseph	Farmer	Middleton
Shaw, Robert	Steward	Colne and Nelson
Stead, Lawrence	Broadcloth merchant	Bury
Tatham, John	Owner of machine works	Rochdale
Taylor, James	Owner of tannery business	Wigan
Taylor, Thomas	Owner of tannery business	Wigan
Thompson, James	Builder and contractor	Blackburn
Turner, Samuel	Farmer	Rochdale
Walker, Robert	Farmer	Middleton

Name	Father's occupation	Location
Ward, Henry	Barber	Blackburn
Watson, Thomas	Mill manager	Rochdale
Whalley, Henry	Foreman joiner	Middleton
Whittam, William	Legal profession	Bolton
Winterbottom, Archibald	Farmer and manufacturer	Manchester
Wood, Thomas B.	Banker	Middleton
Woods, Joseph	Partner in cotton firm	Preston
Wright, Edward	Wine and spirit merchant	Oldham

Entrepreneurs whose parents were from the working classes

Name	Father's occupation	Location
Beads, James	Operative spinner	Blackburn
Dickinson, William	Cotton spinner	Blackburn
Fish, John	Handloom weaver	Blackburn
Haworth, John	Blockcutter	Accrington
Haworth, Richard	Mill worker	Manchester
Higham, Eli	Factory worker	Accrington
Hoyle, William	Factory worker	Bury
Jackson, John	Handloom weaver	Rochdale
Knowles, Mark	Handloom weaver	Blackburn
Lambert, James	Labourer	Accrington
Mallalieu, Samuel	Handloom weaver	Middleton
Mitchell, John	Factory worker	Clitheroe
Porritt, Joseph	Handloom weaver	Bury
Ridings, Thomas	Operative spinner	Preston
Walmsley, John	Handloom weaver	Darwen
Whitehead, John	Quarryman	Burnley

Chapter Six

The Standard of Living on Merseyside, 1850-1875

A. T. McCabe

The standard of living controversy has centred mainly around the period between 1815 and the 1840s, while the middle decades of the century have generally been considered ones of increasing prosperity. This period, from about 1850 to 1875, was a supposed golden age for farmers and craftsmen, but what life was like for the labourers, for those in insecure occupations and for those in the great urban centres is another matter. One way of answering such a question is by the creation of a series of regional mosaics such as this one, concerning the standard of living on Merseyside between 1850 and 1875.

The standard of living attained in any period may be defined as the extent to which the basic physical needs of health, shelter and nutrition are met by the levels of real earnings of the period. Liverpool in the nineteenth century was something of a byword for its mortality and general ill-health; throughout the middle period with which this chapter is concerned, the registration district of Liverpool consistently outstripped all of its major urban rivals in mortality rates by two to three persons per thousand. The registration district of

Liverpool was the parish, the centre of the borough, and, as will be seen later, the unhealthiest part of it. If this is combined with the other registration districts of West Derby, the Wirral and Birkenhead, and these are taken together to represent Merseyside, then the results embodied in Appendix 1 can be obtained.

In only eight years — 1853, 1856, 1859-61, 1872-3, and 1875 — was the death rate for Merseyside below the 1850 level of 27.18 per 1,000 of the population. Expressed as five-yearly averages, the death rate of Merseyside was as follows:

Death rate per 1,000	
1851- 5	28.98
1856-60	26.90
1861- 5	30.79
1866-70	30.97
1871- 5	27.22

The pattern is one of stabilisation in the first half of the 1850s, leading to a definite decline in the second half of that decade; a decline, however, which was arrested and reversed in the 1860s, with mortality reaching its peak in 1866 — a year of cholera — with a rate of 38.97 per 1,000. 1871-5 saw the re-establishment, more or less, of the level of the 1850s, at 27.22 per 1,000. Even so, the closing years of the period by no means exhibited a uniform trend, including as they did the year of lowest mortality in the period — 1873 — as well as one of the worst years — 1871 — with a death rate of 32.44 per 1,000.

The birth rate followed a similar course, rising in the 1860s:

Birth rate per 1,000	
1851- 5	35.12
1856-60	35.37
1861- 6	38.97
1866-70	39.38
1871- 5	37.43

The interaction of the birth rate and the death rate upon each other is not clear: a higher birth rate may have boosted the infant mortality rate, which would obviously be reflected in the overall death rate; or was the higher death rate more a function of overcrowding resulting from a population influx in the 1850s and 1860s? These points must be returned to later.

In the meantime, having considered Merseyside as a whole, its components must be investigated, for it is being used here as an umbrella term for areas that differed sharply in size and density, an uneasy mixture of urban and rural. The borough of Liverpool dominated the surrounding region, with an estimated population in 1850 of 367,000, rising to 517,045 in 1875.

In terms of mortality, the borough in this period divides itself into two areas, exhibiting fairly distinct trends: the parish, and the extra-parochial wards of Everton, Kirkdale, the Toxteths and West Derby. The population of the parish was declining from 1861, after a decade of very slow growth, while that of the extra-parochial wards was increasing rapidly throughout the period; and the latter were a great deal healthier, as can be gathered from table 1. The high point for mortality, as would already be expected from seeing the figures for Merseyside as a whole, came in the 1860s, and the low point in the late 1850s.

Table 1

Five-yearly average death rates and birth rates: borough of Liverpool and constituent parts, 1850-1875

	Death rate			Birth rate		
			(per 1,000 of population)			
Year	Borough	Parish	Extra-parochial wards	Borough	Parish	Extra-parochial wards
1851-5	31.00	34.67	24.04	35.27	34.60	36.59
1856-60	29.08	32.11	23.94	35.54	33.87	38.34
1861-5	33.37	37.52	27.45	38.70	37.15	40.85
1866-70	33.53	39.14	27.49	40.06	37.60	42.73
1871-5	29.50	33.87	25.77	38.03	34.92	40.67

129

The contrast offered by the parish and the extra-parochial wards — parts of the same administrative unit — exhibits the very wide differences in living conditions as reflected by the standard of health which could obtain even in adjacent areas. Only on one occasion — in 1860 — did the death rate in the parish fall below 30 per 1,000; only on three occasions — in 1864, 1866 and 1871 — did it go above 30 per 1,000 in the extra-parochial wards. Even so, the latter, for all that they presented much the healthier picture, were generally above the national average in terms of mortality. After a promising opening to the period in 1850 and 1851, the death rate rose markedly in the extra-parochial wards and never fell to the 1850 level again; and it is interesting to note that the epidemics were not confined to the lower parts of the town — the effects of cholera for instance were registered quite clearly in 1854 and 1866, while typhus was reflected in the increased rates of 1863-5 and 1871.

Moving further away from the centre of Liverpool, conditions appear progressively healthier, as can be seen from the five-yearly averages for West Derby, the Wirral and Birkenhead:

Table 2

Five-yearly average death rates and birth rates:
West Derby, the Wirral and Birkenhead, 1850-1875

	Death rate		Birth rate	
	(per 1,000 of population)			
Year	West Derby	Wirral and Birkenhead	West Derby	Wirral and Birkenhead
1851-5	23.94	18.81	36.12	34.62
1856-60	22.61	19.24	36.67	37.19
1861-5	26.43	22.74	40.05	41.47
1866-70	27.22	21.82	41.05	38.63
1871-5	24.96	20.62	39.03	37.34

West Derby registration district, it should be noted, overlaps with the borough of Liverpool, but includes small townships and villages further out to the north and south of it.

These are altogether, then, a more salubrious set of figures, particularly those for the Cheshire registration districts, which fall, in the main, below the national average of around 22 per 1,000 throughout this period. These areas were achieving a considerable surplus of births over deaths, and again the greatest mortality occurred at the same time as the most prolific birth rate, in the 1860s. Not surprisingly, 1866 was the unhealthiest year, with death rates of 33.14 per 1,000 in West Derby and 25.5 per 1,000 in the Wirral and Birkenhead. It is significant that neither area managed as low a death rate in the last five years of the period as for the first five years. Perhaps this was a reflection, in part, of the extra pressures being placed upon medical services and on housing and sanitation in these areas by a growing population — rising from 153,279 to 342,925 in West Derby and from 57,157 to 102,607 in the Wirral and Birkenhead. How far the death rate was a function of population growth and overcrowding, however, is not clear; the parish of Liverpool, with a declining population after 1861, was at the same time undergoing dramatic death rates. There are so many factors to be taken into consideration: perhaps the stock or the quality of housing was diminishing faster than the population in the parish, or perhaps medical facilities were being attracted to the suburbs rather than to the poorer parts of town.

The distribution of deaths within the population according to age can be equally as significant an indicator of the standard of health as aggregate mortality rates. Appendix 2 illustrates the very high infant mortality rate of the period; at its peak in the 1860s, for instance, a new-born baby ran a one-in-four risk of being dead before it reached one year of age. The overall higher death rate in the 1860s is reflected in each age group, although only marginally so amongst the 5-20 year olds (who were by far the healthiest section of the population) followed by the 20-65 year olds. It is interesting that the over-65 age group has more or less interchanged with that of the 0-5 group by the end of the period, in terms of

131

mortality — in 1851-60 death rates in the two age groups were respectively 83.31 per 1,000 and 101.47 per 1,000, while by 1871-80 the rates were 101.17 per 1,000 and 84.33 per 1,000 respectively. The second oldest group, the 20-65 year olds, also experienced an increase in mortality in the decade 1871-80 as compared with 1851-60. In addition, there are changes in the percentage of deaths in the two older age groups to total deaths — from 32.93 to 36.33 per cent in the 20-65 group, and from 8.91 to 10.78 per cent in the 65-plus group between 1851-60 and 1871-80. This is despite the fact that both these age groups represent a declining proportion of the total population — from 53.85 to 52.37 per cent in the former, and from 2.95 to 2.75 per cent in the latter. Each of the three lower age groups benefited from this shift upwards in mortality: as a percentage of total deaths, the deaths in the 0-1 group fell from 24.94 to 23.75 per cent between 1851-60 and 1871-80; in the 0-5 group, from 49.19 to 44.78 per cent; and in the 5-20 group, from 8.97 to 8.11 per cent. At the same time, each of these groups increased as a percentage of the total population.

The decline in mortality in the 1860s, however, tends to make comparisons over the three decades somewhat disjointed. One could, for instance, point to a decline in both the overall death rate and the infant mortality rate in the decade 1871-80, as opposed to 1851-60, as clear evidence of an amelioration in living conditions throughout the period; but a glance at the figures for the interceding decade, 1861-70, would quickly counteract this assumption. One could also question whether the 1860s were a 'rogue' decade in a trend of overall improving mortality on Merseyside, or were more significant as an indication that the urban masses, at least in Liverpool, did not reap the benefits of the undoubted expansion in trade and industry which marked the mid-nineteenth-century economy until the 1870s. Was it, in fact, the comparatively healthy years of the late 1850s which were exceptional?

One point which can be gone back to here is the extent to which the higher death rate of the 1860s was a function of the correspondingly higher birth rate. While the infant mortality rate was higher in the 1860s, the same could be said for the other age groups; and the actual percentage of deaths to total deaths in the 0-1 and 0-5 age groups fell between 1851-60 and 1861-70. It was only amongst the 20-65 year olds that there was a rising percentage of deaths to total deaths in 1861-70, perhaps reflecting that the major epidemics of that decade, cholera and typhus, were not especially diseases of infancy and early childhood, as was scarlatina for instance. Thus, even accounting for the distortions caused by the higher death rate of the 1860s, the burden of mortality in this period on Merseyside appears to have been becoming more evenly distributed among different age groups, and there is no evidence here that the *increase* in the overall mortality in the 1860s was, particularly, a function of the infant birth rate.

Of course, Merseyside as defined here embraces areas of often widely diverging social climates, but the infant mortality rate was disproportionately high in each of the registration districts. The lowest was 150.67 per 1,000 in the Wirral and Birkenhead in 1871-80, and the highest was 305.43 per 1,000 in Liverpool in 1861-70; the respective overall death rates in these two cases were 19.36 per 1,000 and 38.62 per 1,000. The high infant mortality rate must, in part, have been a reflection of the scarcity of medical resources in this period. A rough guide to the availability of medical care on Merseyside in this period can be seen from table 3:

Table 3

The number of physicians and surgeons in the borough of Liverpool and the registration districts of the Wirral and Birkenhead

	1851	1861	1871	1881
Physicians and surgeons	317	305	479	592
Persons to one physician and surgeon	1,366	1,717	1,246	1,155

The position in 1861, with 1 doctor to 1,717 persons, was by far the worst. This may have had some connection with the higher death rates of the 1860s; certainly it was unfortunate that the number of doctors in proportion to the population seemed to be smaller at the very time when the pressures on medical facilities were about to increase.

Apart from the availability or otherwise of sufficient medical attention, three major factors can be listed as possibly contributing to a high death rate: inadequate sanitation, drainage, etc.; overcrowding; and low nutritional status.

The poor sanitary state of Liverpool, in the 1840s in particular, is well known from the Reports to the Sanitary Commission, so that the amelioration of death rates in the 1850s was brought about, in part, by the administrative and financial reaction against the sanitary and zymotic nightmare of the 1840s. The investment in social capital, in terms of expenditure by Liverpool's Health Committee in the years 1848-58, was impressive: £630,000 on paving and flagging, etc.; £300,000 on sewerage, etc.; and £210,000 for removing nuisances and other purposes. The cost of improving Liverpool's water supply in the 1850s was calculated at around £1½ million.[1] The number of sewers constructed in the borough of Liverpool between 1847 and 1860 was 177,525; the number of houses drained, 45,781; and the number of gullies constructed and reconstructed, 10,087.[2] There seemed to be a fair measure of justification for stating in 1858 that 'in every direction an air of progress manifests itself'. This investment and activity was going no small way towards a firmer regulation of the urban environment on Merseyside, but even when Liverpool was experiencing its lowest mortality of the period it was recognised that 'in large towns there must be a limit to the beneficial effects of these operations',[3] which was a prophetic statement indeed in view of the subsequent high mortality of the 1860s.

It is significant that Drs Parkes and Sanderson, writing of Liverpool in 1871, thought that: 'The infantile remittent (enteric) fever does not in ordinary years cause any considerable mortality, while the diarrhoeal affections are not excessive. This probably indicates that *both the drainage and the water supply are fairly good.'*[4] Undoubtedly, the sanitary reforms that took place in Liverpool after 1847 were a vital part of the progress of the area, but the improvements effected in this sphere may have partly obscured the fact that there were other causes, and a variety of circumstances, behind the high mortality and sickness endured by many sections of the population — causes set deep in the economic and social order of the day.

For instance, if housing and overcrowding are considered, is there evidence of amelioration? From the number of persons per inhabited house in each of the areas (table 4), it can be seen that there was an improvement in every case, but the ratios of around six persons to each inhabited house, as obtained in 1881, are still very high.

Table 4

Number of persons per inhabited house in the Merseyside registration districts, 1851-1881

Registration districts	1851	1861	1871	1881
Liverpool	7.32	7.28	6.95	6.64
West Derby	6.12	6.05	5.06	5.70
Wirral and Birkenhead	6.27	5.71	6.13	6.09
Merseyside	6.75	6.53	6.24	5.98

The figures for Liverpool are very high throughout, although there had been a fairly noticeable improvement by 1881. These figures have their drawbacks; by not taking into account house sizes and various other factors, they can only act as the roughest guide. What they probably do represent are highly concentrated pockets of overcrowding and, especially in the Wirral and Birkenhead, the existence of larger houses in the outlying areas.

135

If the number of houses erected in the borough of Liverpool between 1850 and 1875 (table 5) is considered, there is a notable lack of response early on — in 1850-1 — to the intense pressures put upon Liverpool's stock of housing by the Irish immigration in the late 1840s.

Table 5

Number of houses erected annually in the borough of Liverpool, 1850-1875

1850	420	1860	1,549	1870	1,241
1851	837	1861	1,250	1871	—
1852	1,136	1862	1,516	1872	1,559
1853	924	1863	2,015	1873	1,071
1854	829	1864	2,400	1874	1,266
1855	1,355	1865	1,496	1875	1,495
1856	1,708	1866	1,098		
1857	1,520	1867	—		
1858	1,717	1868	—		
1859	1,758	1869	1,209		

Of the houses erected in the borough between 1841 and 1870, a total of 46,109, only 6,473 (14.03 per cent) were classified as for rental of £12 or under per annum. The cost difficulties involved in any attempt to erect dwellings for the labouring classes in Liverpool, at a profit, were considerable:

> The area of ground required for a single house would cost £2 14s per year, and the cost of building the house cannot be taken at less than £90 which, even at the low rate of 5%, makes the cost to the owner £4 5s, which, without the risks of being unlet and other contingencies, is a rental of 3s per week. The rates and taxes cannot be taken at less than 6d per week, making in this hypothetical case a rent of 3s 6d which would be one-fifth of the income of a labourer of the class we are dealing with, or twice as much as custom considers the proper proportion.[5]

Under these circumstances, apartment dwellings and

sub-letting on a large scale were inevitable. Just how large a scale was shown when a sub-let register was set up by the medical officer of health in Liverpool in 1866. In 1867 there were 2,435 sub-let houses on it, and by the end of 1868 there were 6,267. It was only really when the principle of subsidised local housing was accepted and implemented that this problem could be anywhere near solution, and this was a step which, in general, lay outside this period. One effort was made by Liverpool's local authorities to supply dwellings in this period with the erection of St Martin's Cottages in 1869, with proposed rentals ranging from 3s to 6s 6d per week for 146 families. The next such project came in 1885 with the erection of tenements in Victoria Square, but it was not really until the 1900s that the erection of more than the isolated block of corporation tenements and houses in Liverpool was begun.

Progress in housing may have been limited, but what of the nutritional status of the population? National per capita consumption figures for most foodstuffs increased during this period,[6] and although the use of per capita consumption statistics does have pitfalls, it would appear to establish that the food supply was expanding in the middle decades of the nineteenth century. The distribution of this increase is, of course, another matter, and even amongst the working classes there could be considerable divergence in dietary patterns — notably between the skilled artisan and the unskilled labourer, often in varying employment. The diet of the poor could certainly be sparse, for instance in 1864:

> The diet of the poor of Liverpool, of the class of paupers, and of those whose earnings are precarious, does not include meat except sometimes on a Sunday; fish is more commonly got; cheese and bacon seldom. Bread is the staple of their food; those a shade better off get butter or treacle with it. . . there are multitudes of people of families not getting parish relief, as well as those who are, whose daily food consists at every meal of tea and bread, bread and tea.[7]

137

Unfortunately, there are no systematic dietary surveys extant for Liverpool and Merseyside in this period. Thus, any discussion concerning diet in Liverpool and Merseyside in 1850-75 must, of necessity, be less than thorough. From dietary surveys in other areas, we know that in the diet of the urban working classes in the nineteenth century the staples were, not surprisingly, bread and potatoes, and that the intake of meat, fats and milk tended to be low. Thus, carbohydrates supplied most of the calories.

Although institutional dietaries are untypical as they do not reflect a free-choice situation, they are worth looking at, particularly as they reflect what was considered at that time to be adequate or inadequate from a dietary point of view. Breakfast was usually porridge and buttermilk, two pints of the former and one pint of the latter for an able-bodied man in the 1860s in the Liverpool workhouse, while children up to seven years generally had bread and sweet milk. Supper was also the same every day, normally a gruel of porridge with bread.[8] Dinner was the only meal that varied from day to day but even then the same meal might recur two or three times a week. In 1869 the weekly dinners for able-bodied paupers were as follows: Sunday and Thursday, 4oz of cooked meat, ¾lb rice; Monday and Friday, 1½ pints of pea soup and 6oz bread; Tuesday and Saturday, 1½lb of scouse; and Wednesday, 6oz of bread and 1 pint of cocoa. Other classes of inmates received much the same, only less of it. Infants were usually put on a special diet authorised by the workhouse medical officer: in 1862 ⅓ pint of fresh milk, 2oz of best bread, and ⅓oz of sugar were given to all those under two years of age at every meal.

While the authorities might be satisfied with 'sufficiency without waste', some of the inmates of the workhouse were far from satisfied, as can be gathered by the following extract from a letter by an inmate to a local journal, the *Porcupine,* in 1870:

> . . . and as to the food, the dinners are merely an apology
> for the same, every man here goes to bed with a hungry
> stomach . . . since the introduction of the reduced dietary
> [1869] the murmuring and complaints of the men have
> been bitter and continuous.

There were various reasons why the workhouse was such a
shunned institution, but it does seem that the food served in
it was a significant one. This does not mean that the poor
could obtain a better diet outside the workhouse, but it does
help to illustrate that level of diet which they thought was
inadequate and unsatisfactory.

In the final analysis, however, it was the movement of real
earnings that dictated dietary standards, and living standards
in general. Appendix 3 shows a cost of food index based on
prices in Liverpool between 1850 and 1875. There are two
notable omissions in this index — tea and sugar — which both
fell in price in this period: a fair quality congou was retailed
at about 3s 4d per lb in 1850, and at 2s per lb in 1875; the
wholesale price of sugar fell from 65s a cwt in 1835 to 26s a
cwt in 1884. The index, however, is limited to those items
for which there is a full series from 1850 to 1875. The
inclusion of these two items would obviously depress the
index — to the extent of about five points throughout — but
even so, tea and sugar are no substitute for any of the
other, more solid foodstuffs — at least not from a nutritional
standpoint.

To return to Appendix 3, it can be seen that it always cost
a household more to feed itself after 1851, sometimes exces-
sively so, as in 1854, 1867 and 1872-3, which were years of
exceptionally high bread and potato prices. The index of
contract prices of white bread in Liverpool reached 164 in
1854 and 1867 and 145 in eight years during this period
(with 1850=100). Meat prices rose the most consistently
throughout the period, reaching as high a level, on an 1850-
based index, of 183 in 1873 and 1874. Thus, to even maintain

the fairly modest level of meat consumption of 1lb per person per week of 1850 throughout the period would have necessitated either fairly substantial economies in other spheres or a significant increase in earnings.

Not every item, however, on this index exhibits a consistent upward trend: eggs, potatoes and milk occasionally fell below the 1850 level, and all items fluctuated in price a great deal. The inflation of the early 1870s is most marked, while there is something of a deflation in the late 1850s and again in the late 1860s. The overall upward trend between 1850 and 1875 is, nevertheless, undeniable. Thus, unless the cost of rent, food and clothing declined drastically, a marked increase in earnings would have been necessary simply to maintain a household's standard of living at the 1850 level. But contract prices, at least of cloth and coal, tended to rise in this period: grey cloth per yard was 3s 4½d in 1850, and 3s 8d in 1875; boots, which were 10s a pair in 1864, were 12s a pair in 1875; slack coal was contracted at 4s 6d in 1865 and at 9s in 1875. Contemporary evidence as to movements in rents — as may have been gathered from what has already been said on housing and overcrowding — points to their having increased in this period.

Of course, a full price index must include all these other items as well as the cost of food, but here the cost of food index on its own can be safely used as a basis for translating wage rates into real wages. Comparable wage data on a local scale for this period can be difficult to obtain, particularly for unskilled occupations. From the sources available, however, some series for real wages can be constructed as shown in Appendix 4. These figures differ markedly from the national movements in real wages as calculated by G. H. Wood,[9] which were 20-30 per cent above the 1850 level in 1875. They are not necessarily representative, possibly reflecting more stable rates of money wages than would be normally found, and, of course, both groups of workers represented — engineering workers and printers — belonged, more or less, to the labour aristocracy. However, they do give grounds for modifying Wood's calculations which have for so long been the basis for assessing the standard of living in the second half of the nineteenth century.

There appears to have been little increase in money wages up until 1870, and there may have been a decrease in the late 1850s. Speaking of the engineering trades in 1861, Thomas Brassey stated that: 'In this trade it is an undoubted fact that since 1852 there has been practically no augmentation whatever in wages earned by operatives.' In the case of engineering workers in the Canada Works, Birkenhead, money wages, with 1854 as a base, fluctuated only narrowly until 1869, when the series ends. The printers' and compositors' money wage index rose only twice in this period, from 100 to 103 in 1865, and from 103 to 113 in 1875. Other trades appeared to follow the same pattern of fairly stable wage rates until the early 1870s; for instance, the average money wages of house joiners and carpenters in Runcorn between 1866 and 1875 were as follows: 1866-71, 28s (100); 1872-4, 30s (107); and 1875, 33s (113). Average wage rates in the building trades on Merseyside, with 1860 as a base, were 99 in 1859 and 100 in 1860-2, 137 in 1877 and 127 in 1880; average wages in gas works on Merseyside did not alter between 1855-6 and 1859-62, and by 1880 had risen by 30 per cent.[10] It is legitimate, therefore, to conclude that the money wages of skilled workers in particular were rising on Merseyside in the 1870s after a long period of stability, but these increases did not appear to be enough to combat the sharp rise in food prices of 1872-3.

It is more difficult to establish movements in the wages of the unskilled labourer. The average hourly wages for labourers in various trades in Liverpool and surrounding neighbourhoods is given below for a number of years after 1855. The series, based on the same wage census of 1886, unfortunately breaks off in 1862, to resume again in 1877.

The Standard of Living on Merseyside, 1850-1875

	1855-9	1860-2	1877	1888
Average wage per hour	3½d	3¾d	4½d	4¾d
Index (1855-9=100)	100	107	129	136

The increase in the 1860s compares favourably with the money wage index for skilled workers, which appears to have remained stable at that time. Even so, the evidence here supports the supposition that wage rates did not increase more than moderately, except perhaps in the 1870s. It cannot, therefore, be assumed there was any rise in real wages on Merseyside for the bulk of the period 1850 to 1875.

Altogether there are certainly grounds for reconsidering the view of this period as being one of amelioration in living conditions and of an increasing standard of living. Of course, it may be said that Liverpool was an exception, in terms of mortality in particular, but even in healthier areas, such as the Wirral and Birkenhead, death rates were higher in the five years 1871-5 than they were in 1851-5. It may be said that perhaps the poor did not benefit from the economic expansion of this period, but that the better-off workers did; yet the real wages of skilled workmen such as those in the engineering trades in Birkenhead do not encourage such an assumption for Liverpool and Merseyside. The alteration in real wages brought about by allowing for unemployment shows the degree to which earning potential could be damaged in slumps. This can be seen particularly in the engineering trades: in 1858 and 1866-9 the real wage index, as can be seen from Appendix 4, was considerably deflated by high levels of unemployment — 6.22 per cent in 1858 and 4.55, 8.78, 7.69 and 5.72 per cent in the years 1866-9.

The effects of unemployment in general could be catastrophic — in the slump of 1857-8 Liverpool's labouring population experienced the most extreme distress, as described in the annual reports of the Liverpool Domestic Mission Society:

> I believe that seldom have the poor had to endure such
> hardships as fell upon them in the awful winter of 1857
> to 1858. There were cases of the most fearful character,
> and all the ordinary appliances of the poor law fell far
> short of the requirements of the sufferers.

The effects moreover were not just shortlived: 'The debts of
the winter hang about them, and they are fortunate if in the
spring and summer they can earn sufficient to pay off the
scores that have accumulated against them at the provision
shop or in their rent books.'

The downturn of the trade cycle in 1866 is also reflected
in the domestic mission's reports for that and subsequent
years; work was slack in the shipbuilding yards, in engineering, and on the docks. The following is a breakdown of thirty-
two families relieved by one worker of the domestic mission
in November 1866:

> The heads of these families I have classified as follows:
> fourteen, or nearly one half, were employed in the
> shipbuilding yards, either as skilled workmen or mere
> labourers; seven were labourers on the dockside; four
> carters; three employed at Horsfall's forge; two widows
> with families, and not in receipt of parish pay; one a
> sailor's wife without monthly payment; and one a
> coach trimmer.

The years spent at or near the peak of the trade cycle may
have been ones of improved standards of living for the bulk
of the population, but slump years were still felt very keenly,
as in 1857-8 and 1866-7. In many years, particularly in the
1860s, death rates were disturbingly high, and epidemics — of
cholera, typhus, scarlatina and smallpox — were still a matter
of course. Taking into account the trends in mortality and
living conditions and the insecurity engendered by cyclical
unemployment, together with the rising food prices and
stable wage rates of the period, it must be concluded that

there is little evidence which points to an improved standard of living on Merseyside between 1850 and 1875.

Notes to this chapter are on pages 189-90

Appendix 1
Vital statistics of the combined Merseyside registration districts of Liverpool, West Derby, the Wirral and Birkenhead, 1850 to 1875

	Estimated population	Total deaths	Total births	Death rate per 1,000	Birth rate per 1,000
1850	456,152	12,397	16,433	27.18	36.03
1851	468,672	13,766	17,084	29.37	36.45
1852	479,352	13,750	16,544	28.68	34.51
1853	490,032	13,019	16,280	26.57	33.22
1854	500,712	15,975	17,873	31.90	35.70
1855	511,392	14,402	18,279	28.36	35.74
1856	522,072	13,650	18,830	26.15	36.07
1857	532,752	15,147	19,501	28.43	36.60
1858	543,432	16,273	18,956	29.94	34.88
1859	554,112	14,238	19,662	25.70	35.48
1860	564,792	13,713	19,104	24.28	33.82
1861	575,467	15,434	20,000	26.82	34.75
1862	586,342	16,450	22,623	28.06	38.58
1863	597,217	18,550	23,489	31.06	39.33
1864	608,092	20,729	24,693	34.09	40.61
1865	618,967	20,981	25,734	33.90	41.58
1866	629,842	24,548	25,328	38.97	40.21
1867	640,717	18,410	26,045	28.73	40.65
1868	651,592	18,832	26,002	28.90	39.91
1869	662,467	18,625	25,033	28.11	37.79
1870	673,219	20,305	25,802	30.16	38.32
1871	684,219	22,194	24,970	32.44	36.49
1872	697,579	17,375	26,946	24.91	38.63
1873	710,939	17,031	25,903	23.96	36.43
1874	724,299	20,953	27,722	28.93	38.27
1875	737,659	19,068	27,532	25.85	37.32

Appendix 2
Age distribution of average annual mortality in the three decades 1851-60 to 1871-80 on Merseyside

Ages	Average population per annum	% of total population	Average deaths per annum	% of total deaths	Average death rate per annum (per 1,000 of population living in each age group)
1. 1851-60					
0-1	15,941	3.05	3,592.1	24.94	225.34
0-5	69,820	13.37	7,084.6	49.19	101.47
5-20	158,740	30.41	1,292.0	8.97	8.14
20-65	281,102	53.85	4,743.2	32.93	16.87
65+	15,408	2.95	1,283.6	8.91	83.31
Total	522,050	—	14,403.4	—	27.59
2. 1861-70					
0-1	19,513	3.10	4,695.4	24.35	240.63
0-5	85,512	3.58	8,979.0	46.56	105.00
5-20	193,488	30.72	1,665.3	8.63	8.61
20-65	335,932	53.34	6,840.7	35.47	20.30
65+	16,079	2.55	1,705.2	8.84	106.05
Total	629,822	—	19,286.4	—	30.62
3. 1871-80					
0-1	23,235	3.09	4,598.5	23.75	197.91
0-5	102,817	13.69	8,670.6	44.78	84.33
5-20	234,288	31.20	1,570.0	8.11	6.70
20-65	393,278	52.37	7,033.5	36.33	17.88
65+	20,637	2.75	2,087.9	10.78	101.17
Total	751,020	—	19,362.0	—	25.78

Appendix 3
Cost of food index for Liverpool, 1850-75

(1850 = 100)

1850 — 100	1860 — 129	1870 — 121
1851 — 100	1861 — 130	1871 — 129
1852 — 109	1862 — 132	1872 — 147
1853 — 119	1863 — 124	1873 — 160
1854 — 140	1864 — 114	1874 — 143
1855 — 135	1865 — 127	1875 — 127
1856 — 134	1866 — 136	
1857 — 130	1867 — 141	
1858 — 124	1868 — 126	
1859 — 123	1869 — 123	

Weighting: An estimated weekly consumption of a family of five (man, wife and three children) of: 27lb of bread; 26lb of potatoes; 5lb of meat; 2lb of salt butter; $3\frac{1}{8}$lb of oatmeal; 7 eggs; 1 gallon of new milk. Based on W. Neild, 'Income and expenditure of working class families in Manchester and Dukinfield', *Journal of the Royal Statistical Society* 4 (1841), 320-34.

Appendix 4
Real wages on Merseyside
(1850 = 100)

	Printers and compositors[1]		Engineering workers[2] (Canada Works, Birkenhead)	
	Real wages	Allowed for unemployment	Real wages	Allowed for unemployment
1850	100*	98	100*	—
1851	100*	98	100*	—
1852	92*	90	92*	—
1853	84*	82	84*	—
1854	71*	69	71	71
1855	74	72	74	73
1856	75	74	75	73
1857	77	75	77	76
1858	81	79	78	73
1859	81	80	78	77
1860	78	76	78	78
1861	77	75	77	75
1862	76	73	76	74
1863	81	78	81	78
1864	88	87	89	88
1865	81	79	80	79
1866	75	74	77	73
1867	73	71	74	67
1868	82	79	79	73
1869	85	83	66	62
1870	85	82	80	78
1871	80	78	—	—
1872	70	69	—	—
1873	64	63	—	—
1874	72	71	—	—
1875	87	88	—	—

*Estimates

Sources: (A) Wage rates:
      [1] Based on printers' wage rates given by A. L. Bowley and G. H. Wood, *Journal of Royal Statistical Society* 62 (1899), 708-15.
      [2] T. Brassey, *Trade Unions and the Cost of Labour* (1870).

    (B) Unemployment:
      [1] Board of Trade, *Statistical Tables and Charts* (1909) (C-4954) Section X (Table 103).
      [2] *Annual Reports* of the Amalgamated Society of Engineers, Birkenhead Branch.

Chapter Seven

The Liverpool Police Force, 1836-1902

W. R. Cockcroft

Liverpool's reputation in the first half of the nineteenth century was such that it was known as the 'Black Spot on the Mersey' because of the extent to which crime and violence prevailed in the dockland and city areas. And yet the port, being ideally situated for maritime trade and passage, expanded alarmingly during these years, becoming a magnet for workmen from all parts of Britain and, in particular, Ireland. While many saw it as the 'Gateway to the West', Liverpool's resident population more than doubled between 1801 and 1831, with a further increase of 80,000 between 1831 and 1841. It was hardly surprising, therefore, that the old municipal organisation of the port began to collapse, and that the forces of law and order with which this chapter is particularly concerned should have proved inadequate to deal with the increased volume of crime.

Until 1836 Liverpool possessed three independent constabulary forces — a corporation day force under the town council; a night or town watch under the Commissioners of Watch, Scavengers and Lamps, and a dock police under the Dock Committee — all of whom had low standards of health, education and general organisation, and between whom there was often serious rivalry.

The night watch was an ill-organised, inefficient and inadequate body of officers and men, notorious for their heavy drinking and fighting among themselves and for bullying citizens on Saturday nights. Captain Morrow, described as a typical watchman, 'sometimes breaks out drinking and continues it for two or three days — on these occasions he reports himself to be taken suddenly ill'.

The day force was also lazy and corrupt. Some of its members would accept bribes, desert their beats, ignore fights or drink on duty, while their preference for the fires of their lock-ups was well known. One of them was almost carried off to Ireland while in a drunken condition. This force patrolled only as far as the parish boundaries, and in 1833 only four of its members were responsible for Toxteth Park and Harrington — an area with a population of 25,000.

The dock police, formed in 1815, were the most efficient force of the three, owing in no small measure to the appointment of M. M. G. Dowling, a former London police officer, as their superintendent in 1832. An autonomous force, they were completely incorporated into the new borough force only in 1841.

In an attempt to remedy this situation the corporation of Liverpool made a start in 1830 by recruiting a Lieutenant Parlour from the metropolitan police, who introduced metropolitan methods into Liverpool and reorganised the night watch according to the then revolutionary principle of selection by merit. The night watch, together with the day police, then formed the basis of the new Liverpool Police Force which was formed in February 1836. Its first head (or chief) constable was Michael J. Whitty, at that time superintendent of the night watch, who was responsible to the newly appointed Watch Committee.[1]

Following the metropolitan plan, Whitty separated the borough into two main police districts by drawing a line from Water Street, along Dale Street, up Shaw's Brow and directly up Low Hill. In the north his men operated from the Exchange Street East and Vauxhall Road bridewells, and in the south from the Brick Street and Duncan Street North bridewells. Each division (which was under a superintendent) was subdivided into eight sections (with an inspector in charge of each), and then into beats. Of the 360 men who made up the new force, no less than 114 had served in one or other of the previous forces. Each constable now worked an average of twelve hours a day, seven days a week, for which he received eighteen shillings a week. Some of them, moreover, had extra duties to perform as town firemen.

The prime concern of the police was, however, to establish law and order by 'preventing' crime. An attempt can be made to assess their effectiveness in achieving this by looking first at the major threats to law and order, and then at the individual records of the five head (or chief) constables of Liverpool.

Major threats to law and order

The first constables who set out to patrol Liverpool faced major problems of juvenile delinquency, drunkenness and prostitution, as well as 'depredations' from the thousand known male thieves, the five hundred others who 'stole at intervals', the six hundred others operating from the docks and the estimated twelve thousand lads under the age of fifteen in their employ.[2] Crimes of violence were also numerous, owing in part to the ever increasing number of steam vessels bringing sailors into the port. Quayside violence in particular gave Liverpool an evil reputation, and the frequent cases of stabbings were encouraged by the common practice among sailors until the 1860s of carrying a sheath dagger. In 1856 the number of recorded stabbings was 185, mainly committed by persons when drunk. Added to this were the outrages perpetrated during municipal elections and between Orangemen and Catholics, as well as the additional problems of crowd control, demonstrations, and organised strikes. Each of these can now be considered in turn.

The many thousands of abandoned, neglected or homeless children without education or occupation who roamed the streets of Liverpool were one of the largest problems that the police had to face in the mid-century.[3] Introduced to crime at an early age, they soon progressed (if unchecked) to the ranks of the professional criminal. Hundreds of them regularly lounged around 'the singing saloons' or low theatres such as the Sans Pareil, the Liver, the Queen's Theatre, the Custom House or the Penny Hop. Visiting the latter, Captain Williams, the Inspector of Prisons, discovered that:

> the streets . . . and the avenues leading to it are occupied
> by crowds of boys . . . it consists of a spacious room
> fitted up in the crudest manner, with a stage and seats on
> an inclined plane. The access to it is through a dark passage
> and up a ladder staircase. On one occaion I was present, I
> found the audience to consist almost exclusively of boys
> and girls of the lowest description, many without stockings,
> and to the number of 150. . .

Crowds of them also visited the travelling fairs where they saw coarsely presented scenes of crime and bloodshed such as *The Murder of Maria Marten in the Red Barn*. Captain Williams estimated that all theatrical performances at this time were calculated only to 'familiarise the mind of youth with vice'. Even twenty years after the force was formed such places as the Williamson Square Free Concert Room, the Lord Nelson Street gambling halls, the Royal Casino near the docks and the Salle de Danse Theatre, as well as boxing, dog-, rat- and badger-fighting public houses, were still plentiful.[4]

The criminal activity of the majority of these children consisted of petty pilfering, mainly from the shopkeepers and street traders who exposed merchandise of all kinds, but also from the docks. Vandalism was also rife. Until the middle of the century these juveniles, once in court, were sentenced to punishment similar to that of adults: even for stealing food they could be sent to the local Kirkdale County Prison (replaced by Walton Gaol in 1855) or to the Borough Gaol in Howard Street.

An act of 1847 ensured the more speedy trial of juvenile offenders in order to avoid the corrupting effects of their association with adults before trial. This was achieved by giving the magistrates powers to deal summarily with simple cases and to limit sentences to three months' imprisonment. Some Liverpool boys thus found their ways to industrial schools (such as the Philanthropic Institution in Surrey, the Dalston Refuge in Middlesex or the county refuges at Chester and Edge Hill), being sent there on a free pardon, conditional on attendance. Others were sent to 'feeding schools', where they received some education and training in a trade.

In 1854 there were further improvements when existing reformatory schools were given grants subject to Home Office inspection. After that, courts could sentence boys to detention in reformatories at the end of their period of imprisonment. The industrial schools were also put under government inspection, and magistrates were authorised to send to them children who were homeless, found begging or frequenting the company of thieves, or beyond parental control.

The Liverpool Watch Committee thus constantly made attempts to remove children from the sources of crime. They sought legal powers to visit brothels and remove child inmates — especially very young girls. Their efforts were not always appreciated, however, when, for example, the *Liverpool Review* for 22 August 1885 alleged that dock constables freely used canes against 'wretched, half-starved and ragged children'. In fact, police work for needy children — especially between 1880 and 1900 — was outstanding: they sent children found begging to the Islington Children's Shelter and effectively enforced the Prevention of Cruelty to Children Act of 1899, as well as the legislation to protect children from

licensed premises and street-hawking. Head Constable
Nott-Bower welcomed these efforts at a time when 'the dirt
of the delinquents, the swarm of vermin and possible disease'
made the disinfection of juvenile prisoners a very difficult
task for his men. He also helped to found the Liverpool and
Bootle Police Orphanage in 1895, in which year the Liverpool
Police Aided Clothing Association inquired into the cases of
4,532 insufficiently clothed children, particularly from the
docklands.

Chronic public drunkenness[5] was the second major threat
which constantly undermined the peace, and it gave the
Liverpool police more than half their work. In the 1830s
there were estimated to be no less than 1,200 public houses,
beer houses, taps, gin palaces and penny ale cellars in the
borough, and from one point near the Vauxhall Road bridewell it was possible to count twenty-seven such premises.
Furthermore, the Beer House Act of 1830 permitted free
trade in beer, so that any person whose name was on the rate
book might open a beer shop on payment of two guineas to
the local excise office. In this way there opened in Liverpool
more than eight hundred beer shops in the nineteen days
following the introduction of the act on 10 October.

Little could be done for many years because the combination of licensing laws and local business interests did little
to check drunkenness. Early Tory-dominated city councils
favoured the brewing interests, and often forced the head
constable — via the watch committee — to safeguard public
house licences. The Liberals on the other hand were often
bigoted, and in their zeal for the temperance cause took little
heed of police experience. The police themselves were
seriously handicapped by the local magistrates who,
encouraged by the brewers, even went so far in 1862 as to
grant public house licences to virtually anyone who could
show that he had suitable premises. After four years, during
which 336 more houses were added to the previous excessive
total, the experiment was abandoned. Head Constable Greig

also exacerbated the antagonism between licensees and his men by the use of plain clothes officers: in 1857, for example, a magistrate under pressure from the brewers dismissed several informations laid against beer house keepers solely because police officers had made plain clothes visits to the premises.

In an attempt to free the city from heavy drinking a vigorous temperance movement spread throughout Liverpool, the David Jones Society, established in Scotland Road in 1835, being among the first total abstinence branches of the movement in the country. In spite of a licensing act in 1855 which closed drinking places from 2pm on Sundays until 6am on Mondays, it was not until the passing of the Intoxicating Liquor Licensing Act of 1872 that the situation was improved. This necessitated, among other provisions, that public houses be managed in a better fashion, and restricted the sale of alcohol to between 7am and 11am on weekdays, and between 1pm and 3pm and 6pm and 9pm on Sundays, Christmas Day and Good Friday. Employers thereafter found fewer men absent from work, while Sunday mornings became more peaceful, and the town's streets became quieter by night, especially on Saturdays.

Eager for further improvements, many leading Liverpool citizens joined together to form the Liverpool Vigilance Committee in 1875. Unfortunately, the extremists among its members became obsessed with a desire to increase the number of convictions for drunkenness and pressured the head constable into expanding his public house inspection corps. This was a well organised group, with uniformed inspectors and constables in plain clothes, but the scheme was costly and time-consuming, taking experienced men away from more important duties. However, Head Constable Nott-Bower was, after 1881, totally against the system, and although this brought the censure of the temperance party on his head he succeeded in persuading the watch committee to allow him to abolish the special corps and make his superintendents responsible for supervision in their divisions instead.

Following this, the police began to witness a decrease in public drunkenness — from 16,040 convictions in 1892 to 5,305 in 1897. Nott-Bower ascribed this not only to his new system, but also to the closer investigations of the Licensing Bench, the demolition of much insanitary property in the old areas of the town and the clearing of rookeries, the depression of trade in the early nineties, the low level of wages, the growth of football, cycling and other organised sports, the improved facilities for travelling to and from work (whereby men reached their destinations without stopping to drink), the discontinuance of the practice of 'subbing' wages (ie of pay clerks advancing small amounts), the increased strictness of the benefit societies with regard to men who drank to excess, the general improvements in education, and, finally, the closing of many unlicensed drinking houses. The police, however, recognised that the decrease of prosecutions for drunkenness did not necessarily mean a proportionate increase in temperance.

Prostitution[6] was the third major problem with which the Liverpool police had to contend and which, like the liquor problem, could become a burning issue at local election time. With the docks flush with Yankee clippermen, Liverpool-Irish 'packet-rats', 'China Birds' and Negro sailors, several areas of the port became notorious for soliciting. In particular, prostitutes plied their trade in the sailors' quarters which spread from Lancelot Hays through Castle Street and the back streets, from Wapping to Park Lane and Paradise Street, reaching as far as the lower end of Parliament Street and its neighbouring side streets and, eventually, moving as far as Lime Street in the very heart of the city.

In 1837 the Constabulary Committee estimated that there were 520 brothels in Liverpool with an average of four prostitutes in each, together with 625 houses of ill fame and 136 common lodging houses also used by them. In this way Liverpool became one of the most notorious centres for prostitution outside London, with young girls of Irish parentage being commonplace. Captain Williams noted that, out of a sample of women committed in 1864, 605 were 'Protestants' and 921 Catholics: many were not twenty-six or -seven years old, but had already been imprisoned between thirty and sixty times. He found them 'creeping alive' with vermin in 1837, and ten years later they could still be found 'lying like pigs doing nothing . . . in gaudy clothes torn and soiled with blood and dirt, the effects of drunkenness and quarrelling'. Venereal disease was common-place among them, and as late as 1880 it was estimated to account for 4.3 per cent of all patients in Liverpool hospitals.

When they endeavoured to tackle the problem of prostitu-tion the police were handicapped by the law, as for many years they could arrest these women only if they were found annoying other people. The brothel-keeper too could be prosecuted only if he kept a disorderly house. Some towns in Britain -- mainly those with large military camps — were subject to the Contagious Diseases Act of 1864, whereby rigorous checks were made of suspected or known prostitutes. Liverpool, however, remained free from this law, and prostitu-tion increased unchecked, although official figures for 1861 and 1871 noted only 686 and 764 known prostitutes respectively.

So openly and shamelessly did these women solicit that proposed solutions to the problem tried either to attack it at its roots by attempting to improve the social and economic conditions that gave rise to it, or alternatively to suppress it by indiscriminate prosecution and severe punishment.

An example of the first approach was Josephine Butler, who began to take prostitutes into her own home when she arrived in Liverpool. Originally intending to improve conditions in the Liverpool workhouse, she developed her campaign into a national one for moral purity and for the abolition of the Contagious Diseases Act. Some Liverpool merchants helped her to establish an industrial home for girls in 1867, where they learned laundry work or worked in a small envelope factory.

In contrast, the Liverpool temperance party agitated for sweeping reforms to remove the ill repute attached to the name of Liverpool, many of its members failing to consider the more practical methods of achieving reform. Hence, the problem of Liverpool prostitutes caused the greatest friction between the head constable and the temperance party. With their powerful spokesmen in the Liberal party, the latter fought several municipal elections on the question of vice.

In November 1890, when the Liberals won control of the council, the head constable was forced against his own better judgement to follow their orders. They argued that, because it was an offence to keep an immoral house, the police should close all known brothels and that constables should 'clear the streets of prostitutes'. Though Greig and Nott-Bower had, by close supervision, gradually reduced the number of brothels to 443 in 1890 and confined them to certain districts — thereby preventing them from spreading — this did not deter the Liberals. Nott-Bower vehemently opposed this policy because he argued that brothels would always exist for a large seafaring population and that an attack would scatter them into respectable districts.

As a result of the Liberals' policy, 443 informations were laid, one against each Liverpool brothel known to the police. This action shocked public sensibility, led to extreme harshness and generally impeded moral reform. As predicted, it did much to spread prostitution into respectable neighbourhoods and among innocent people, and supervision became extremely difficult. Nott-Bower's men noticed many more prostitutes using common lodging houses, entries, passages and other places to which the public had easy access. Fortunately, after a special meeting of council in 1896 to consider the entire question, a return to the pre-1890 system was recommended.

Preserving the peace was another of the most difficult tasks confronting the Liverpool police. In June 1841 for example, some 20,000 people attended an anti-Corn Law Association meeting, in preparation for which Head Constable Whitty had concealed 300 men in nearby St John's market. Although he managed to prevent any serious trouble, mobs of Irish labourers started a series of attacks which lasted for two days. Later in the same month, he had to rescue the town from a similar outbreak during the three-day parliamentary election.[7]

At the root of these troubles lay the Irish immigrants, who by the mid-1840s were overcrowding the workhouses, lodging houses and police stations. Daily fights and brawls were commonplace in the poorer districts of the town, and only the arrival of the police curtailed 'scenes of constant up-roar and bloodshed'.

In such an atmosphere the authorities were anxious to avoid an anticipated clash with the Chartist supporters in 1848. They called in the militia, enlisted the help of various other police forces, had the Liverpool police drilled with cutlasses and had one hundred picked men trained with carbines. They were never called upon however, for Chartism never caught on in Liverpool.

With much merchandise carelessly exposed for long periods on the quaysides, the docks were also the scene of numerous larcenies. Dockside thieves became so troublesome that in 1865 a river police department of about twenty men was formed to prevent 'crimping' or shanghaiing. They were badly handicapped for years, however, because they had only three small rowing boats or 'gigs', which were frequently involved in accidents — as in 1868, when the constables of a capsized boat were only just saved by two Mersey lifeboats. By the nineties however, crimping had largely disappeared and this work of the force was wound up.

On land the police had a new phenomenon to face as many strangers from outlying districts flocked into the city on Sundays as a result of the cheap fares provided by the Railway Act of 1844. On 13 July 1845, for example, 5,300 trippers arrived at an early hour from Manchester, and a week later 7,000 more caused overcrowding in the leading thoroughfares from Edge Hill station to the docks from early morning until midnight. Large numbers also embarked on vessels bound for the Mersey Light Ship and back.

Organised strikes presented another serious problem for the Liverpool force. Unemployment was a perennial problem, so that when dockers struck in February 1879, for example, the local militia had to be called out. Such economic unrest was common in a city with such a high proportion of un-skilled workers — not only Irish, but also German and Italian.

Dangerous Fenian outbreaks also had to be faced during these years. In February 1867, Head Constable Greig's prudent action in speedily despatching information which came to his attention prevented Fenian attacks in Chester and Dublin. The climax of their violence in Liverpool came in 1881 when they attempted to destroy the town hall and the Hatton Garden police station. Their bomb exploded in the lobby of the police house — a residence for young constables — but although much damage was done, it was confined to the entrance portion.

Nott-Bower also had his share of violent crises. For example, he had to investigate the allegations in the *Liverpool Review* of June 1886 that dangerous and highly organised 'High Rip Gangs' were terrorising dockers and executing vengeance on all in Scotland ('D') Division who gave evidence against them. This scare continued until Justice Day put an end to it by having all those prisoners who were convicted for robbery with violence at the assizes on November 1886 flogged with twenty or thirty lashes in addition to their sentence. Needless to say, this had a stunning effect on 'D' Division.

Head constables of Liverpool

It is with such major threats to law and order in mind that the records of the individual head constables can be reviewed. With the majority of the population apparently opposed to the formation of the borough force in 1836 (as in other places at this time) Head Constable Michael Whitty (1836-44)[8] had perhaps the hardest task of any head constable. He had no experience to guide him, and met serious difficulties in obtaining suitable officers and recruits. It says much for him that he succeeded in gradually overcoming these difficulties.

Whitty's strong sense of discipline probably resulted in his early training for the Catholic priesthood. Impulsive but kind, he had a tenacious memory, and was said to be able to call every man in his force by name and rank. That he set out to discipline his new charges with untiring zeal was due perhaps in no small measure to the fact that, when attacked by a mob in July 1835, he was rescued by two bystanders rather than by watchmen. For a long time afterwards he had 200 cutlasses stored for police use in the main bridewell.

Continually short of qualified manpower, Whitty had yet to build up the morale of the force. Badly paid and on call at any time, his men also had to live where they were told. Some of the Catholic-Orange antagonism even penetrated his force. He must then have been disappointed, if hardly surprised, to find that out of the original 360 men recruited in 1836 only 172 were still in the force by 1838 — although this was similar to the experience of other large towns at this time. Nevertheless, when he left the force after eleven years' service he had soundly established it on a firm basis.

His successor was Henry Miller, who came to Liverpool with an excellent record of eight years' service with the Glasgow police, but he stayed in Liverpool for only eight months. Appointed on 12 August 1844, he resigned on 26 October, after being asked to do so by the daily board of the watch committee, who accused him of being too haughty and overbearing with his senior officers. It was also said that he drilled his men too harshly, and that he marched prisoners through the town chained by ankle fetters. Matters came to a head when Miller flagrantly flouted the authority of the watch committee. Birkenhead had asked for his services and the help of fifty men, a request that was denied by the Liverpool watch committee who felt that Miller was needed to keep order among large crowds at the pier heads. Nevertheless, Miller crossed the river at 7 am and did not return until 3 in the afternoon — having taken the chief fire officers with him as well.

When Miller accepted the chance to resign the *Liverpool Mercury* took his side, and in doing so touched on the question of who had the ultimate authority over the borough constabulary — the watch committee or the head constable. The Municipal Corporations Act of 1835 was surprisingly silent on the issue, the watch committee taking their powers from those sections of it which empowered them to make regulations 'for preventing neglect or abuse, and rendering constables efficient in the discharge of their duties', with the provision to dismiss any constable 'whom they shall think negligent in the discharge of his duty'. But this remained an unresolved question, never tested in a court of law.

Miller's successor, Matthew M. G. Dowling (1844-52) witnessed not only a critical period of Irish immigration but also the expansion of the towns and their docks on an unprecedented scale. Dowling was an experienced head constable, being a barrister-at-law and a Liverpool police commissioner at the time of Miller's resignation, and a former metropolitan police officer. However, his career was cut short by his dismissal from office in 1852 following an attempt by him to preserve his unblemished record by removing a portion of a constable's report from an official report book.

Before his dismissal Dowling had carried his force through a very difficult period. From 1 January to June 1847 an estimated 300,000 Irish landed, 60-80,000 of whom located themselves in the already overcrowded lodging houses and cellars of the town. Moreover, Dowling showed in the police returns for that year that the great increase in crime was caused largely by these immigrants, daily fights and brawls being common in the Irish communities. In all, an estimated one million Irish landed in Liverpool between 1849 and 1853.

Conditions for Dowling's policemen were still harsh, and it

was only in 1845 that they received their first pay rise since 1836 — of two shillings a week. Each constable worked an average of ten and a half hours a day, exclusive of his attendance in court, at drills and for pay. No leave was granted until 1860, when it was only thirty-three hours every sixteenth day. During 1846, 168 constables were reported for drunkenness.

It was alleged that Dowling's successor, Captain John Greig (1852-81) was over-dignified, but this was simply an official front, as in fact he was very personal in his approach to his men, and regularly visited the police detainees at the main bridewell on Saturday afternoons. On other occasions he would reprimand those brought in for drunkenness and violence, or those who appeared dirty and unshaven on 'clean shirt day'. But Greig was not only very popular with his men, but highly competent as well.

Obviously the physical expansion of the town at this time did much to overburden the force. Between January 1857 and October 1859 some 4,737 houses as well as numerous warehouses and factories were built in the borough, whose population increased by 30,000 during this same period. And yet Greig was granted only twenty extra constables to cope with this expansion. Hence he resisted a proposal to reduce the military cavalry force of 110 men and the infantry force of 135, both quartered at Liverpool's North Fort.

Several of Greig's policies were noteworthy, particularly his development of the detective department, and the distribution of police aid to the needy. During the severe winter of 1861, for example, they issued some 9,000 bread tickets, 6,720 soup tickets, 275 coal tickets and 50 rugs.

This was also the period when the police had to safeguard the many civic functions of the new city, such as the opening of the William Brown Library, the Museum, the Walker Art Gallery and St George's Hall. Greig also had to face the growing threat of strikes during his period as head constable. He and his men coped well with several potentially dangerous strikes, although the local militia had to be called in when the dock labourers struck in February 1879. He was also asked by many outside forces for police aid, such as in November 1867, when he was unable to send the requested hundred men to help the Salford police at the execution of the Fenian 'Manchester Martyrs'.

Greig held the head constableship of Liverpool with distinction for almost twenty years, and was succeeded in 1881 by Captain John William Nott-Bower (1881-1902).[9] Nott-Bower knew when he accepted the post that the port was notorious for violence. For several years after his appointment the number of reported cases of stabbings and woundings amounted to 250 each year, whilst the number of cases of common assault stood at 2,000. According to Nott-Bower, there were streets in the Scotland Road division which were unsafe for respectable persons to enter and which even the police could not patrol alone. Here, too, petty larcenies were high. The tension was further increased, moreover, by the High Rip Gang rumours.

When the city boundaries were extended in 1895, Nott-Bower transformed the two cumbersome police divisions into five smaller ones. This was entirely necessary because his men had to patrol an area that had increased from 6,524 to 15,252 acres. They had to safeguard 399 miles of streets, compared with their former 277 miles. The population had increased from 503,967 to 642,095 and the rateable value from £3,203,000 to £3,787,226. To cope with these new demands, his force was expanded from 1,294 men to 1,460.

Much of his early work, such as the formation of the mounted police in 1886 and the initiation of the police ambulance and patrol wagon systems, prepared the ground-work for the large-scale reorganisation of the force in 1895. When the three patrol wagons purchased in 1891 were linked by the use of private telephones to the bridewells, Nott-Bower took his example from the United States. These horse-drawn vehicles, with a removable stretcher at their centre for carrying violent prisoners, usually carried three constables but could carry ten when the need arose. In time, they helped quell the noisy city brawls and obviated the vulgarity of constables dragging violent prisoners through the streets. This mobilisation of his men stemmed from his, Nott-Bower's, success with the police ambulances. Appalled by the callousness shown by ignorant stretcher-bearers in the removal of people who had met with accidents in the streets, he drew up plans for an improved system with Reginald Harrison, a barrister-at-law. At their instigation the Watch Committee in 1882 supplied eighteen of the police and fire stations with two-man wheeled ambulances. With nineteen four-man stretchers already in use in the city, each district of Liverpool had some humane means of conveyance for the injured.

In the main, therefore, Nott-Bower's constables were hard-working, although they did come in for severe criticism with the mismanagement of the general store in the Hatton Garden police section house in 1888. Exaggerated newspaper reports — initiated by the *Liverpool Citizen* in October 1888 — condemned the store as a police boozing den. After careful investigation, however, it was found that some non-members of the force and non-resident constables had been supplied with beer, but there was no evidence of disorderly conduct.

In contrast, his men distinguished themselves on numerous occasions, notably during the visit of Queen Victoria from 11 to 13 May 1886, when she opened the Liverpool Exhibition. Their record of duty on this occasion was remarkable as they actually performed the equivalent of four and one half days' work in two days. Though much of this was undertaken in very bad weather, their admiration for the Queen was enthusiastically shown on the thirteenth when, at their request, they were allowed to remove their helmets and join in the cheers of the crowd as she passed.

In view of his fine record, Nott-Bower was elected on 21 March 1902 to the commissionership of police in the City of London. He thus left the greatest police command in England outside the Metropolis, which had seen many changes since 1836. The new comprehensive force removed much of the notoriety associated with the name of Liverpool throughout the world. Nevertheless, the force still had weaknesses, as when the head constable became the servant of a politically motivated watch committee.

The constables, too, had their grievances. Their duty was extremely arduous and pay and holidays still poor. Poor rates of pay induced many policemen to quit after a short term of service. This inevitably led to moments of crisis, as in 1896 when constables produced a petition about their pay. In 1836 they had had to work continuously without leave during the week or on Sundays: by the end of the century every member of the force was granted thirty to forty days' leave, and more if his health suffered. By this time, however, the constable had fewer days' rest than the average Liverpool citizen, who by then relaxed at least on Sundays, Saturday afternoons and bank holidays. In spite of this the force did increase from 360 men in 1836 to 1,804 in 1900, while over the same period of time the population increased from 246,000 to 668,000. Several of the head constables created new and impressive departments, but the streamlining of the force's structure was not uniform.

Was it surprising then that so many policemen either re-signed or were dismissed? Many of the early constables were ignorant, heavy-drinking men only seeking temporary employment, who quickly succumbed. Nevertheless, the head constables did manage to improve the standards of the men. Throughout the century the lamentable number punished for committing offences while on duty was substantially reduced, so that Nott-Bower was able to report that, whereas 21.2 per cent of the men were reported for offences in 1879 (12.3 per cent being 'the worse for liquor'), only 6.8 per cent were reported in 1899, 3.8 per cent of these having been found in a drunken state.

The constables also improved their educational standards.

This was probably general throughout the United Kingdom, but special measures had been adopted in Liverpool. As late as 1885 the majority of the force was illiterate, many even of the higher officers being unable to write, much less spell, a short report. By the end of the century, a chief inspector was instructing each recruit not only in writing, spelling, arithmetic and the preparation of reports, but also in the theory of police duty. Before promotion, each man had to pass a searching examination. Instruction in first aid, swimming and life-saving, drill and gymnastics was also systematically imparted to recruits.

The professionalism of the new force greatly discouraged wrongdoers and proved a contributory factor, together with social and economic improvements, in reducing known crimes in Victorian Liverpool. Charles Dickens highlighted this efficiency when he wrote in *The Uncommercial Traveller* that the 'Liverpool Police Force is composed without favour of the best men that can be picked [and] it is directed by an unusual intelligence'.

Compared with other borough forces, therefore, the Liverpool constabulary was outstanding. The success of the new police in the city forced many lawbreakers to change their habits. Many, according to Nott-Bower, must have given up their old ways; some hardened criminals even moved beyond the city boundaries. In general, therefore, the number of known lawbreakers diminished by the end of the century and Liverpool's public places became safer for the ordinary citizen to frequent — especially after dark.

Notes to this chapter are on page 190

Chapter Eight

Victorian Entertainment in the Lancashire Cotton Towns

M. B. Smith

Much has been written about the economic and social conditions of the working classes in the Lancashire cotton towns in the nineteenth century but less is known of their entertainments and pastimes, even though local newspapers, journals, directories and biographies provide a rich source of such information.

During the first thirty years of the nineteenth century there had been an extension of working hours and thus a gradual encroachment into the free time of the factory worker, but between 1833 and 1853 those in the textile industry achieved a ten and a half hour 'normal' day, with Saturday afternoons free. Although this was not universal in all trades and occupations, growing urbanisation and the increasing number of workers subject to factory discipline meant the gradual acceptance of working hours which were more regular, if shorter. All of this helped to change the value of traditional forms of leisure and to influence the development of new activities. Thus by 1830 the traditional holidays were reduced to Christmas Day and Good Friday, fairs continued (but with little of their original significance), and 'wakes' had different values in different towns. The regular leisure hours of evenings and Saturday afternoons grew in importance.

Among the more important leisure activities in the early years of the nineteenth century can be included the mechanics' institutes, which developed during the twenties and thirties but whose activities occupied relatively few of the operative classes, together with the activities of temperance societies from the thirties onwards. Public house entertainment was, understandably, of wider appeal, but so was the theatre, which was always popular in the cotton towns, and musical activities — especially brass bands. From the thirties onwards the railways provided new horizons for working-class leisure, so that, while Sunday entertainment was never a positive feature in any of the cotton towns, it was possible to find entertainment elsewhere.

Thus although the traditional forms of leisure activities continued, these were modified during the mid-nineteenth century to meet the changing demands of the new industrial working classes. After 1871 in particular a more regular and distinct pattern of holidays emerged with the introduction of an increased number of statutory public holidays and the widespread achievement of a five and a half day week. This meant that the working classes had more time and opportunity to follow a wider choice of interests than in 1830. To illustrate this point, this chapter will examine two popular forms of entertainment — the theatre and the fair — as these reflected the economic and social changes taking place in Victorian Lancashire.

There were permanent, established theatres in Preston, Blackburn, Bolton and Oldham during the 1820s, and although these were small and unpretentious by later standards, they did provide a wide variety of classical and contemporary drama, pantomime and opera. For example, the Theatre Royal in Preston had been built for the guild celebrations of 1802 but a theatre had existed on another site before that date. Other Lancashire towns had less permanent sites for theatrical performances, and assembly halls and inns were used instead. In this way *Richard III* was staged at the Bull Inn, Horwich in 1832 and the *Hunchback* at the Swan Inn, Chowbent in the same year.

Theatrical productions during the 1820s reflected the attitude of a pre-industrial society to leisure, although the theatre was already being influenced by the changing social structure of the cotton towns brought about by the increasing numbers in the factory wage-earning class. During the twenties the theatre was almost completely associated with the lower-middle and middle classes of the towns. John Taylor, an amateur actor from Bolton, looking back to the 1820s wrote:

> The theatre at Bolton was then open on Monday, Wednesday and Friday. Seldom was the same piece repeated. The receipts of the theatre during three nights a week enabled the manager to pay his servants fair wages and were quite equal to the present overdone system of cheapening prices and reducing the quality of the plays by overtasking the energies of the actors and filling the houses with factory lads and lasses for whom the theatre was never intended.[1]

From this it can be inferred that during the twenties there were usually no weekly programmes, and that most of the theatres were open on three or sometimes more weekdays; but Saturday night was no special occasion. Furthermore until 1843 the establishment of theatres and the type of performance given was under the strict control of the Crown, so that the Drury Lane, Covent Garden and Haymarket theatres in London were the only ones supposedly producing plays without songs or dancing in the programme. This restriction was no handicap for the productions in the Lancashire towns, where an evening's entertainment at the theatre was usually divided into three parts. A typical performance before 1843 was that given in Preston in August 1826 when the Theatre Royal staged *A Cure for Heartache* by T.

Moreton, 'a truly excellent and laughable comedy', followed
by a group of songs, the performance concluding with 'the
celebrated farce' *Rendezvous, or Love in all Corners.* Theatre
performances during the twenties, thirties and later usually
began at 7pm which prevented the factory operatives and
many apprentices from attending a full performance. Since
most productions were very lengthy, half price was usually
offered after 9pm when the cost of a gallery seat was 6d. The
comic intervals between two plays became a popular feature
with the audiences in the gallery, and it was these variety acts
which were later developed into complete performances
during the 1840s. The *Preston Chronicle* noted in 1829 after a
performance at the Theatre Royal:

> After the play and some comic singing, the gallery were
> in ecstasies at the appearance of two men monkeys,
> 'Jocko and Jacko'. We were glad to see Mr Taffre alight
> without injury on the stage after a most daring journey
> with Monsieur Gouffe round the upper boxes and gallery.

The growing demand for working-class entertainment
was met only in part by this sort of variety entertainment
staged in the theatres and assembly rooms, so that the
public houses in the expanding industrial towns also
played a major part in developing this form of entertainment. The inns and taverns in town and country districts
had always been concerned in staging a variety of pastimes and sports and were the centres of many social,
political and trade clubs at all social levels. They remained
important centres for leisure activities throughout the
nineteenth century, but some enterprising landlords
widened the scope of their entertainment to stage various
forms of variety productions.

Local singers and fiddlers were well known in the
Lancashire public houses. John Harland, in his *Ballads
and Songs of Lancashire,* writes of an Oldham man who
in the early years of the nineteenth century came to

Gorton wakes every year to sing in three public houses in that village, and of another, 'Parish Jack — a singer, fluter and fiddler — in great request at stirs and merry making'. When, as a result of the Beer House Act, some 190 beerhouses were set up in Preston alone between 1830 and 1834, even some of these now provided 'entertainment'. Thus John Dunlop, an advocate of temperance, was in no doubt that the publicans organised entertainment to attract customers, and in doing so created a serious social problem.

> Publicans use all manner of schemes to allure and attract
> by means of games, music, getting up country wakes,
> bull baiting, quoit playing, bowling, wrestling, running,
> boxing, horse racing, card playing, skittles, Dutch pins,
> bumble puppy, drafts, dominoes and other entertainments.
> And the intimate and inseparable connexion in this country
> between these amusements and drinking is most disastrous
> and an astonishment to other nations.[2]

His views did not upset the publicans or deter the growing demands for entertainment, as the inns were concerned with all levels of cultural activities. Thus in 1837 the Bolton Philharmonic Society was practising 'every Thursday night at the large room of the Levers Arms Hotel which was elegantly fitted up for that purpose'; the Accrington Choral Society in its early years met at the Black Bull assembly room of the Red Lion Inn, while the Blackburn Choral Society met at the Angel Inn, King Street.

In the early forties, some larger public houses began to have a 'music hall' or 'singing saloon' attached to their premises, to provide a variety form of entertainment and also serve food and drink. This was an attractive alternative to theatre entertainment where no drink was served. Tom Sharples, the owner of the Star Inn at Bolton,[3] who owned a museum attached to the inn as well as a music hall, advertised his evening entertainment in the museum catalogue of 1845:

> Then when the shades of evening draw near,
> Again the scene is changed your hearts to cheer;
> Music and mirth inviting bids you stay,
> Softens rough hearts, and makes the sad ones gay.
> Makes old age young, brightens the brow of care,
> Chaseth devils blue, and grim despair.
> The Star of Bolton is the guiding light
> To music — mirth — museum day and night.

In 1855, when the inn was rebuilt after being destroyed by fire, the landlord offered as an evening's entertainment a string and brass band, madrigal singers, comedians, a Negro melodist and histrionic sketches. There were many types of 'saloons' and 'halls' catering for all tastes, and the landlord set the tone as well as often acting as chairman for the night's entertainment.

For the growing numbers of young men and independent wage-earning young women between the ages of fifteen and twenty-five the 'singing saloon' seems to have been a popular meeting place on Saturday night, especially for the wilder section of the poorer classes. Many of these places were considered disreputable and at best as providing doubtful entertainment for the factory worker. They remained popular with young men and women throughout the sixties and seventies, but there was considerable opposition to them from middle-class critics, particularly during the fifties and sixties. In the *Northern Monthly* on 15 March 1862 it was reported:

> It is not in concert halls, though professedly devoted
> to music for the millions, that one finds the real
> working classes, or learns what is the sort of musical
> entertainment that has the greatest attraction for the
> lower strata of the people. It is the singing saloon that is
> characteristically theirs.

Writers admitted that the comforts of the saloons were attractive alternatives to the dimly lit, overcrowded, poorly furnished room that served as a home for many poorer people, but all writers condemned the entertainment. For example, the *Northern Monthly* in 1862 described one of them as follows:

> A large room having pretensions to elegance well lighted and well warmed, a crowd of working people, male and female, many of them of a seemingly decent sort, others very suspicious, others plainly dissipated and bad. Beer and tobacco — things that have their legitimate use — are here partaken freely under circumstances that invite the abuse of them.
>
> At the upper end of the room are the preparations for a musical performance, a piano, a seedy gentleman with a violin, a remarkably easy and assured but debauched looking young man who sings comic songs and one or more female singers, prodigal of their poor and faded charms.

The Rev John Clay, the chaplain of Preston gaol during the 1850s, was a very stern critic of the saloons and was concerned with their degrading effects:

> The child rejected or outraged at home soon finds in the streets or fields companions in misery and idleness. Petty thefts were ventured or bolder ones planned and effected; then arises the inclination for debasing excitement and it is plentifully supplied by low theatres and singing saloons.

Despite attempts to wean the working classes from the snares of the singing saloon by the provision of cheap popular concerts, they remained a popular form of entertainment.

> [They are] attended by our sabbath scholars, by the young lads of respectable families and by young women who are to be wives and mothers of a large and important class of our town population.[4]

In the same paper a prison inspector suggested that the saloons were popular with boys at quite an early age. He commented on a 'notorious singing saloon' in Bolton where 'all the thieves and bad characters of the town are to be found. In that saloon on Saturday night may be found no fewer than five hundred boys under or about the age of fifteen years.' The price of admission was 2d and it entitled the holder to some refreshment.

The simpler, more traditional form of public house entertainment, however, remained. These were often billed as 'Free and Easies' or 'Harmonic Meetings', such as those held at the Wellington Inn, Deansgate, Bolton, during the forties, where every Saturday and Monday the proprietor presided over the meetings, providing piano accompaniment for the singing. On Sunday evenings he offered sacred music. Advertisements for this type of entertainment were careful to suggest that strict order and social comfort would be preserved. At the Albion Inn, Sweet Green, Bolton, the proprietor seemed rather more ambitious: he offered amusements of a 'musical and social character' in his 'elegant and commodious' place of entertainment.

Different forms of 'free and easies' were presented in many different types of public houses and remained popular with all classes. Many provided enjoyable meeting places and combined 'chit chat on passing events and leading topics of the day with classical and popular music both vocal and instrumental'.

The advertisements again seem to suggest that many of these entertainments had a predominantly male following. In 1868 a writer reporting on a 'free and easy' concert at the Old Cock Inn, Preston, noted that there were forty gentlemen present, with 'excellent singing and a brass and string band'. The chairman remained an important feature of this type of entertainment: loud and amusing, he encouraged the audience to link with the entertainers and take an active role in the evening's proceedings.

Before the rapid expansion of the cotton towns the ballad singer and street performer had played an important part in the entertainment of the towns and villages; but with the rapid increase in the number of work people involved in factory production during the thirties and forties their roles as entertainers declined. The ballad singer had been a newsman whose ballad sheets formed an important part of the reading of a large section of the community. Several writers during the fifties complained of the decline in the number of street ballad singers and blamed the growing number of concert rooms and music halls. But the attitudes to work and leisure had changed; a 'normal day' had been achieved, towns had local papers and better communications, and the ballad singer reached only a small proportion of the town population. Street performers continued their trade, but they were not always welcome. The ballad singers continued to be a feature of the country towns which were the main circulation areas of the ballad sheets; in the cotton towns, however, the penny song books had become more important by the 1860s. Professional artistes in singing saloons and music halls gained in popularity with the increasing numbers of penny song books which were being printed.

Parallel changes to those taking place in the music halls attached to inns were already occurring in the theatres during the forties. In January 1848 Cora, Jumba, Woski, Miami, Yarico, Womba and Rosa appeared at northern theatres. At the Theatre Royal, Preston they were billed as:

> Young ladies whose immense success in London at St.
> James Assembly Rooms has been made a theme of
> eulogy by the public press. Female American seranaders.
> Vocal and instrumental music. Introducing their most
> favourite and popular overtures, glees and songs.

The public was reminded that 'performances began at 8pm and carriages were ordered for 10.30pm'. The show was so

successful it was retained for two further evenings. The
audience was invited to participate in the performance by
buying the song book, so that the association between songs
and particular singers became a feature of the performances
in the music hall theatres of later years. Many of these shows
appealed to all social classes and were accepted as respectable.
A report in the *Preston Guardian* for 13 January 1848 stated:

> Picturesquely attired and by the aid of some pigment
> or other, their faces assumed a very hot copper colour.
> They accompanied themselves with banjos, bones,
> triangles, etc. The taste for nigger melodies in this
> town must be very great for on Monday evening every
> part of the house was crowded and hundreds, it is said,
> went away unable to gain admittance.

During the fifties and later, Negro and minstrel shows were
very popular and 'Christy Minstrels', 'Old Original Christy
Minstrels', 'Butterworth's Christys' and 'American Christys'
toured the northern theatres. These shows, and the varied
programmes of the more respectable music halls, had a
considerable following from all social groups and resulted
in the building of the large ornate music hall theatres of the
eighties which provided a family entertainment.

By the 1860s the working classes considered the theatre
and music hall entertainment as direct alternatives.

> The theatre is the most popular resort of pleasure
> seeking workmen and the gallery their favourite part
> of the house. Two or three males generally go together
> taking with them a joint stock bottle of drink and a
> suitable supply of eatables . . .
>
> . . . After the theatres the music halls are the most
> popular places of Saturday night resort with working
> men and in them they can combine the drinking of the
> Saturday night glass and the smoking of the Saturday
> night pipe with the seeing and hearing of a variety of
> entertainments.[5]

178

The more sophisticated music halls encouraged respectability, and landlords arranged private entrances to select rooms that had a full view of the stage. In January 1871 the King's Head New Concert Hall in Preston advertised:

> Success defies all. Great concentration of talent for New Year's week. This is the largest and most respectable hall in town. The highest class talent and great novelties are already engaged and nothing will be wanted on the part of the management to make the entertainment worthy of the appreciation of a really respectable audience.

This form of entertainment, which continued into the 1930s, lost some of its earlier vigorous characteristics, but the traditions were firmly centred in the earlier forms of the 'free and easy' music hall and singing saloon entertainment. It was almost 'exclusively working and lower middle-class both as to composers, singers and popular audiences'.[6] From the 1840s onwards a professionalism and commercialism developed which had not been apparent in the amateur-professional relationships of early years. The songs which formed the main part of this kind of entertainment, like the artistes who sang them, grew out of a poor urban environment, and although the songs were not works of art they indicated, with a bitter humour or sentimentality, the everyday life and romantic hopes of the working classes and their relationships with other social groups of Victorian society.

Of all forms of entertainment, the changing nature and value of fairs probably reflected most closely the changing social structure of the cotton towns, with their rapid urbanisation and growing technological progress. All the cotton towns held three or four annual fairs between the years 1830 and 1870. Over this period the fairs changed in character and importance and in later years became less concerned with trading. Moses Heap commented on the local attitude to fairs:

> In my boyhood days we always had our annual procession
> from the National Schools at Crawshawbooth, which
> was held on the first Tuesday in June — and being the
> fair — though it was on a small scale, it all seemed very
> wonderful to us youngsters. . . . All the mills stopped at
> noon for the day and continued to do so until the ten
> hours act of Parliament became law in 1847.[7]

The fair was an important local occurrence, especially during
the first forty years of the nineteenth century, but its character began to change in the Lancashire towns with the spread
of industrialisation. It lost much of its value as the factory
worker gained a normal day with regular and defined leisure
hours. Household goods were still bought and sold during the
thirties, and certain fairs continued to be noted for particular
goods, but Heap commented on the difference between 1830
and 1870: 'This fair [1834] was also noted for housemaids
and old wives laying in a stock of new crockery. Those days
are now a thing of the past.' Change was probably apparent
during the thirties when William Howitt described 'modern
additions' which sold trinkets rather than household goods,
'. . . and through the bazaars, these modern additions to fairs,
goes a perpetual stream of gay people admiring the endless
variety of things that are there displayed on either hand'.[8]

The link between leisure and work in the locality, which
the fair had in many ways strengthened, was broken in the
late forties, when the entertainments it offered were no
longer the only means of pleasure. Commenting on these
changes during the forties, Heap noted that: 'In place of
the fair we see hundreds of workpeople carrying boxes and
bags on their way to the railway station for a few days at the
seaside.' A critic, lamenting the decline in the number of
public holidays in England, suggested in 1853 that 'fairs as
holidays are nothing now to the inhabitants in cities'.

The circuses, menageries and travelling shows combined
together at fairs during the early decades of the nineteenth
century, and although they continued to do so throughout

the century, already by the thirties they were able to arrange complete shows at any time throughout the year. In 1833 Batty's Royal Equestrian circus appeared in Preston on the open ground known as Chadwick's Orchard. This circus was already 'brilliantly illuminated with gas', and the manager pledged himself:

> to produce in the same brilliant and finished manner as at the Liverpool establishment — to effect which he has caused to be transferred from his Liverpool theatre (regardless of the attendant expense and inconvenience) all appurtenances and appendages inseparable from the grandeur and pomp of these performances.

Circuses were popular with all social classes and performances usually began at 7pm. Some of them offered additional attractions, as at Batty's circus where 'ladies and gentlemen [could be] taught the polite art of riding'.

Wombwell's circus toured the Lancashire towns during the thirties. It included a large menagerie of wild beasts, and the performances boasted an excellent band. Pablo Fanque's circus was also on tour during these years. It was an attraction at the Preston Guild celebrations of 1842 (when many children of the Preston day and Sunday schools attended), and appeared in Rochdale in 1843 when the performances were 'under the patronage of the gentlemen of Rochdale cricket and bowling club'.

The circuses and fairs in the cotton towns in the thirties and forties occupied such sites as the market square at Blackburn. There were permanent sites, too — in Mount Street, Manchester a wooden building called Cooke's Circus was built in 1842 to stage equestrian shows. Liverpool also had a permanent site at this time. During the fifties Newsome's circus appeared at the Star Concert Hall theatre in Bolton. There was 'a splendid stud of horses', and 'St George and the Dragon' was produced during the last week of February 1856. These large shows were very

181

popular and appeared at any time of the year. Some of the tented circuses that toured during the thirties were, however, quite small affairs; a few horses, perhaps, a clown, acrobats and a tight rope walker. Fairs were their main pitches, unlike the larger circuses, and they appeared in the Lancashire towns during wakes weeks. The fairs attracted peep shows and freak exhibitions, novelties — goldfish pulling boats in a glass tank, oysters smoking pipes — roundabouts, fortune tellers and gingerbread stalls. Some of the sideshows suffered local criticism when there were 'girls exposing themselves to the public gaze for money like the commonest exhibitors at a theatre'.

From the thirties onwards some of the fairs and wakes were wild affairs and George Sanger, writing of Stalybridge wakes in 1850, commented:

> The wakes were very rough affairs in those days, the
> Lancashire lads and lasses making holiday at them in
> the wildest possible fashion. The clog was their weapon
> and they considered there was nothing unmanly in
> kicking and biting to death — for they would use their
> teeth like dogs — any person who had the misfortune to
> incur their anger.[9]

He went on to describe an attack on the owner of a gingerbread stall: 'From our position on the platform we could see the poor fellow's body with the heavy clogs battered into it as though it was a stuffed sack instead of a human being.'

Of the sideshows, the peep show seemed to be an especially popular attraction. This was simply a large box with a lens in one side through which the customer viewed scenes depicting murders, topical political events, riots or famous battles at ½d per time. With slight additions or alterations the pictures could depict several scenes. At a time when many people were illiterate and the illustrations in magazines were confined to black and white reproductions, attempts to show a record of recent events, however primitive and exaggerated, were welcomed by an appreciative audience.

In later years, during the fifties, the magic lantern was used in sideshows, and scenes painted on glass a few inches square could give a picture twenty feet square using oxy-hydrogen for illumination. In the thirties stallholders, exhibitors and circus entertainers had difficulty in providing adequate lighting at night with rush lights and tallow candles, but during the fifties the use of naptha lights and gas was much more common.

The circus remained popular with all social groups throughout the nineteenth century so that by the 1870s several circuses had very large companies which gave a much more varied performance. Sanger, describing a continental tour that his circus made in 1870, wrote:

> I took forty-six carriages, one hundred and sixty horses, eleven elephants, twelve camels, all sorts of circus accessories and two hundred and thirty people. I have spent eleven summers travelling through France, Germany, Austria, Bohemia, Spain, Switzerland, Denmark and Holland. I have played in all their capitals and have been honoured by the patronage of twelve crowned heads.

This circus appeared in the Lancashire towns during the sixties and seventies, and the *Blackburn Standard* reported on 10 May 1871 that: 'Sanger's extensive circus and Hippodrome took up quarters in the market square. At noon on Monday [it] paraded through the principal thoroughfares with a valuable stud of horses and accompanied by a band.' The interest in circuses in the cotton towns was great enough for another large circus, Swallows, to be touring during the same season. Visiting Chadwick's Orchard, Preston, in 1871 it offered:

> . . . riders, acrobats, gymnasts, contortionists, great troupe of French vaulters and air divers, diminutive

> ponies and educated mules. Miss Swallow on her
> beautiful palfrey, the wonder of the age. Four
> great clowns.[10]

There were individual performers who could thrill and amuse the crowds. Balloonists were entertaining crowds in the early decades of the nineteenth century and a Mr Livingstone was a balloonist at the Preston Guild celebrations of 1822. In 1837 the American Sam Scott was jumping from tall buildings; he leapt into the Irwell from one of the tallest warehouses 'attired in lace drawers, a red flannel shirt and a bladder drawn over the scalp'. Soon afterwards he went to Bolton to jump into the canal from the warehouse of the Old Quay company. (He was accidentally hanged on Waterloo Bridge in London in 1841.)

The developing theatre, music hall and circus entertainments were only a small part of the growing number of activities that became possible after about 1850, with increasing leisure hours and free Saturday afternoons.

Musical and choral societies had always provided popular entertainment in the cotton towns, and then after 1850 the local brass bands created an intense rivalry between different supporters which was fostered by the annual contest at Belle Vue, Manchester. Wrestling, often arranged at the public houses, could still draw large crowds during this period, while boxing matches were locally arranged. Football gradually developed on enclosed pitches and on Saturday afternoons attracted much working-class support. From 1860 onwards cricket was accepted as a working-class game and several leagues developed. The development of town parks after 1850 provided a stage for the brass band concerts, fetes and horticultural shows. Traditional pastimes continued throughout the Victorian era: coursing could attract more participants from the lower classes after the forties, and whippet racing was adapted to meet the demands of the urban working classes.

The rapid increase in the numbers of independent young men and women between the ages of fifteen and twenty-five who could take advantage of the very real gains in leisure time after 1850 was, however, a major influence in the development of new forms of entertainment and new pastimes. If the old traditions and relationships existed after 1870 and pre-industrial pastimes continued, they played little part in the new relationships between leisure and work or in the pastimes and entertainments of the new industrial society of the Lancashire cotton towns.

Notes to this chapter are on pages 190-1

References

Chapter 1 **The Administration of Lancashire** *pp 9-34*
1   This chapter is based on my unpublished thesis, 'The Adminis-
     tration of Lancashire, 1838-1888'. (PhD, University of Manchester
     1968)
2   For the period 1798-1838 see my unpublished thesis, 'The
     Government of Lancashire, 1798-1838'. (MA, University of
     Manchester 1966)
3   These were at Preston, Kirkdale (replaced by Walton Gaol in
     1855) and Salford (replaced by Strangeways Prison in 1868)
4   The county remained responsible for pensions already granted
     and for loan interest and repayments, however, and the Court
     of Annual General Session continued to appoint committees
     of visiting justices.
5   At the time one person was bridgemaster of Amounderness,
     Blackburn, Leyland and Salford.

Chapter 2 **The Making of the Borough of Salford** *pp 35-58*
1   Tait, J. *Medieval Manchester and the Beginnings of Lancashire*
     (Manchester 1904: reprinted 1972), 10. Salford acquired a
     seignorial charter in 1230, Manchester in 1301
2   Greenall, R. L. 'The Development of Local Government in
     Salford, 1830-1853' (MA thesis, University of Leicester 1970), 22-5

3   Lockett, W. *Reports Relative to the New Salford Improvement
     Act* (Salford 1844) and *A Letter to William Lockett . . .
     containing remarks . . . relative to the new Salford Improvement
     Act* (Manchester 1844)
4   London School of Economics, Webb Local Government
     Collection, vol 160
5   Cowan, J. S. 'Joseph Brotherton and the Public Library Movement',
     Library Association Record 59 (1957), 156-9
6   Mandley, J. G. de T. *Broughton: a History of Its Union with
     Salford* (Manchester 1884), 3

Chapter 3   **Baptists and the Working Classes** *pp 59-82*
1   The records of the Lancashire and Cheshire Association of Baptist
     churches are held by the north-west office of the Baptist Union in
     Manchester
2   *Baptist Handbook* (1876), 54
3   Mayor, S. *Churches and the Labour Movement* (1967), 14-15;
     Best, G. *Mid-Victorian Britain* (1971), 182-3
4   Inglis, K. S. *Churches and the Working Classes in Victorian
     England* (1963); Mayor, 13-14; Best, 183-4
5   Harrison, B. *Drink and the Victorians* (1971), 97
6   Smith, F. B. 'The Atheist Mission' in Robson, R. (ed). *Ideas and
     Institutions of Victorian Britain* (1967), 205
7   Hayden, R. (ed) 'Baptists in the Cotton Towns of Lancashire'
     (typescript 1965), 16. For further references see my unpublished
     thesis, 'Baptists in Lancashire, 1837-87' (PhD, University of
     Liverpool 1970)

Chapter 4   **Furness Newspapers** *pp 83-102*
1   Hunt, F. K. *The Fourth Estate* 1 (1850), 2; Andrews, A. *The
     History of British Journalism,* 2 (1859), 347, 348; Grant, J. (ed)
     The Newspaper Press, 3 (1872), 205
2   Lucas, P. J. 'The First Furness Newspapers: The History of the
     Furness Press from 1846 to *c.*1880' (MLitt thesis, University of
     Lancaster 1971). Nine of these papers lasted under three years;
     the *Ulverston Advertiser* over sixty-six
3   *Progress of British Newspapers in the Nineteenth Century*
     (1901), 79, 80
4   Williams, R. 'Radical and/or Respectable' in Boston, R. (ed).
     The Press We Deserve (1970), 23

5 Read, D. *Press and People, 1790-1850* (1961), 68-72
6 Perkin, H. J. *The Origins of Modern English Society, 1780-1880* (1969), ch. 9, and Tholfsen, T. R. 'The Transition to Democracy in Victorian England', *International Review of Social History*, 6 (1961), 226-48
7 Gray, D. L. 'The Uses of Victorian Laughter', *Victorian Studies* 10 (1966), 145
8 Barker, T. C. and Harris, J. R. *A Merseyside Town in the Industrial Revolution: St. Helens, 1750-1900* (1954), 378
9 *Hansard,* 3rd series, 157 (1860), 385

Chapter 5 **The Victorian Entrepreneur** *pp 103-26*
1 Detailed in Perkin, H. J. *The Origins of Modern English Society* (1969), 20-1
2 *The Oldham Journal* (1 March 1884)
3 *The Wigan Observer and District Advertiser* (16 March 1889; 4 November 1896)
4 *The Middleton Albion* (3 June 1893)
5 *The Blackburn Times* (26 August 1890)
6 *The Darwen News* (5 November 1890)
7 *The Textile Manufacturer* (15 February 1884)
8 *The Bury Times* (27 February 1886)
9 Parliamentary Paper 1834, HC 167, p 154
10 Parliamentary Paper 1833, HC 690, questions 9207-15
11 *Manchester City News* (15 December 1883)
12 *The Rochdale Observer* (16 June 1883)
13 *Ibid* (9 March 1887)
14 *Colne and Nelson Times* (18 July 1885)

Chapter 6 **The Standard of Living on Merseyside** *pp 127-49*
1 Liverpool Medical Officer of Health, *Annual Report* (1858)
2 Newlands, J. 'On Sanitary Progress in Liverpool', *Transactions of the National Association for the Promotion of Social Science* (1860), 732
3 McGovern, W. T. 'Sanitary Legislation with Illustrations from Experience in Liverpool', *ibid* (1858), 15
4 Drs Parkes and Sanderson. 'On the Sanitary Condition of Liverpool', part 2, Liverpool Council Proceedings (1870-1), 682 (my italics)

5   Hughes, J. B. and Newlands, J. 'Report to the Sub-committee on Dwellings for the Working Classes', Liverpool Council Proceedings (1864-5), 572

6   Salaman, R. N. *The History and Social Influence of the Potato* (Cambridge, 1949), 613-17

7   Dr Buchan, 'Report upon an Epidemic of Typhus in Liverpool', Appendix to the *7th Report of the Medical Officer of the Privy Council*, Parliamentary Papers vol xxvi (1865), 468

8   Workhouse Committee Minute Books, vol 6 (1862)

9   Wood, G. H. 'Real Wages and the Standard of Comfort since 1850', *Journal of the Royal Statistical Society* 72 (1909), 91-103

10   'Return of Wages Published between 1830 and 1886' in Parliamentary Papers (C.5172) (1887)

Chapter 7 **The Liverpool Police Force** *pp 150-68*

1   The Minutes of the Liverpool Watch Committee (in the Liverpool Record Office) form the major source for this chapter

2   Crime in Liverpool is summarised in Midwinter, E. *Old Liverpool* (Newton Abbot 1971), ch. 3

3   Tobias, J. J. *Crime and Industrial Society in the 19th Century* (1967), 78-92

4   Shimmin, H. *Life in Liverpool* (Liverpool 1856), 11-16; 77-82

5   Harrison, B. *Drink and the Victorians* (1971)

6   Pearson, M. *The Age of Consent. Victorian Prostitution and its Enemies* (Newton Abbot 1972)

7   Cockcroft, W. R. 'The Rise and Growth of the Liverpool Police Force in the Nineteenth Century' (MA thesis, University College of Wales Bangor 1969)

8   *Dictionary of National Biography,* vol 21 (Oxford, 1964)

9   Nott-Bower, Sir J. W. *Fifty-Two Years a Policeman* (1926)

Chapter 8 **Victorian Entertainment in the Lancashire Cotton Towns** *pp 169-85*

Much of this chapter first appeared in the *Local Historian* for November 1971

1   Taylor, J. *Autobiography of a Lancashire Lawyer, being the Life and Recollections of John Taylor* (Bolton 1883), 17

2   Dunlop, J. *The Philosophy of Artificial and Compulsory Drinking Usages in Great Britain and Ireland* (1839), 243

3   For this, perhaps the first music hall in the country, see Mellor,
     G. J. *The Northern Music Hall* (Newcastle 1970), 23-4; plate 1
4   *Tonic Sol Fa Reporter* (14 March 1856)
5   'Habits and Customs of the Working Classes', *Fortnightly Review,*
     n.s. 11 (July 1867)
6   MacInnes, C. *Sweet Saturday Night* (1967), 22
7   Heap, M. *My Life and Times* (1904). Typescript copy in
     Rawtenstall Public Library
8   Howitt, W. *The Rural Life of England* (1838), vol 2, 254
9   Sanger, G. *Seventy Years a Showman* (1926: reprinted 1966), 62
10   *Preston Chronicle* (6 April 1871)

Index